PRAISE FOR *UNFORGETTABLE KNIGHTS*

A great era of Rutgers basketball is described in detail by former Rutgers player Jeff Kleinbaum. He had firsthand experience of this incredible year of Scarlet Knights basketball. It was "Hoops Hysteria" on the campus of Rutgers University.

The team featured a Dynamic Duo in Phil Sellers and Mike Dabney, and they all were so dominant they had the metropolitan area of New York/New Jersey going wild!

Jeff captured the feeling by sharing his insights.

> —Dick Vitale, Former Rutgers Coach and longtime iconic commentator for *ESPN Sports*

During the 1970s, I was fortunate to witness the incredible growth of the Rutgers men's basketball program. Coach Tom Young put together an array of talented athletes who cruised through an undefeated regular season all the way to the Final Four.

The team was composed of mostly metropolitan players.

All of us who coached against this powerful team knew how deeply talented they were. They gave us a sense of pride in our state university team that still resonates.

> —Bill Raftery, former Seton Hall Coach and longtime iconic commentator for CBS Sports

My teammate Jeff Kleinbaum poured his heart and soul into this book and gave us an honorable and authentic account of the Rutgers Final Four team of 1976. This is a must-read for basketball fans and curious minds who want to experience the euphoria of a thrilling, fast-paced journey on and off the court.

Our Final Four team captured the nation's attention and secured our place in history. For me personally, it ranks as my proudest and most emotional achievement, more than winning an NBA championship with the Los Angeles Lakers in 1982 and coaching in the NBA for twenty-plus years.

—Ed Jordan, former Rutgers player and coach and
longtime player and coach in the NBA

Having coached high school basketball for ten years with Jeff (and saved him from numerous technicals), I'm thrilled that he's sharing the riveting, poignant, and even hilarious tales I heard over the years about the fabled Final Four Rutgers team of 1975–76. This book brings to life that unforgettable season and is a must-read as an underdog story for the ages.

—John Harper, SNY-TV and
longtime NY/NJ Sports columnist

Library of Congress Control Number: 2025916713

Paperback ISBN: 978-1-966283-99-7
Hardcover ISBN: 978-1-969063-00-8

　　　1. Main category—Nonfiction › Biographies & Memoirs › Sports & Outdoor › Basketball
　　　2. Other category—Sports & Outdoors › Basketball › College & University
　　　3. Other category—Sports & Outdoors › Miscellaneous › History of Sports

Published by: AR PRESS
Roger L. Brooks, Publisher
roger@americanrealpublishing.com
americanrealpublishing.com

TABLE OF CONTENTS

Foreword by Jerry Izenberg..ix

Introduction..xiii

Wait Until Next Year..1

Destination New Brunswick..5

The Barn..13

The Tumultuous '70s..19

Phil "The Thrill" Sellers..29

Section 1:..36

The Journey Begins..42

The Pressure Mounts...51

Making History..62

The St. Bonaventure Escape / Let the Bell Ring......................72

Phil vs. Beaver..80

Section Two: Team Leadership...88

Destination Philadelphia..97

The Final Four...107

Back to New Brunswick—and Reality....................................118

Threads of Nostalgia:
Fans' Memories from the 1975–76 Season 127

Echoes of Yesterday: My Final Thoughts 143

Section 3: 150

The Final Four Team 150

Whatever Happened to…? 154

1975–76 Roster, Final Statistics, and Results 163

Acknowledgments 165

About the Authors 169

UNFORGETTABLE
KNIGHTS

A Player's Account of the Legendary Rutgers Final Four Season

JEFF KLEINBAUM
WITH TOM LUICCI
FOREWORD BY JERRY IZENBERG

FOREWORD
BY JERRY IZENBERG

A MERICA WAS A BUSY PLACE in 1869. Center stage was the opening of the nation's first transcontinental railroad with the ceremonial driving of the "golden spike," uniting the Union Pacific and Central Pacific Railroads, and Susan B. Anthony founding the National Woman Suffrage Association, the first step toward granting American women the right to vote. Against those headlines, newspapers didn't pay much attention to the news that Rutgers University and Princeton had unveiled a brand-new game called football in November of that year when they played on College Field in the then-sleepy college town (population: 21,000) of New Brunswick, NJ.

College Field never became a shrine for the game that now hypnotizes most of America every weekend. Shrine? Hardly. What it became was the parking lot behind the old gym on College Avenue nicknamed the Barn. From 1869 until 1972—the passage of 103 years—Rutgers did not award a single basketball scholarship. But in the end, it was the Barn that produced Rutgers's greatest single basketball legacy.

What it left us was a Rutgers's basketball season of all basketball seasons—a Rutgers team that played twenty-six regular season games, won them all, and ran the streak to thirty-one on the way to the Final Four in the NCAA tournament.

Until then, Rutgers basketball fans were a congregation of biblical Jobs when it came to patience and loyalty. For all the mediocre basketball games they'd endured year after year in the old building, for all the double dribbles and all the air balls that went the wrong way, they finally got what they never gave up waiting for—the team they had yearned for. And this was *their* team and remains so fifty years later.

It began to take shape when the school president, Edward Bloustein, decided everything has its time, including a move to "bigger time," and he was the man who authorized the first basketball scholarships in 1972 and hired an energetic coach from American University named Tom Young in 1973. It took Young just three years to field the kind of team the loyalty of the fans had earned. Aging paint chips often lost their adherence to the ceiling and rained down on the fan base below, dislodged in flurries as a kind of *a cappella* tribute to the noise they thundered when things went right for the Scarlet Knights.

This was the team Young had fashioned—and, make no mistake, that's what it was: a team. It wasn't Bill Russell carrying the little-known University of San Francisco to back-to-back NCAA titles. It wasn't Larry Byrd taking Indiana State to an NCAA final where it had never been before or since. The 1975–76 Scarlet Knights were in every sense a team…five guys and a twelve-man roster born to play together:

The late Phil Sellers is arguably the best player Rutgers ever had. He still holds the school's scoring and rebounding records fifty years later. Sellers was headed for Notre Dame but changed his mind at the last minute and chose Rutgers.

Mike Dabney was a local star at East Orange High.

Eddie Jordan came out of Washington, DC; Hollis Copeland, a Jersey product from Ewing Township; and James Bailey, the missing piece at center, who played his high school ball in Massachusetts.

Each starter brought something to the table, without whom none of this could have happened. These were the right twelve guys, whose skills complemented each other, playing under a coach who understood each of them. How well he understood is best illustrated by one particular practice when Sellers and Copeland got into a physical confrontation. The root cause was something all five starters shared—the need to compete and to prove who they were.

"Fine," Young told them. "You wanna fight? Go fight. But get off my floor right now. You go on down to the locker room and fight all you want."

They left and talked and realized they weren't even mad at each other. They returned to the gym, sat in the stands, and watched what was left of practice. The spur for the fight had been their need to compete. Sellers was a six-foot-four power forward who generally matched up against bigger opponents, but he still averaged 19.2 points and 10.2 rebounds a game as a senior. Copeland's explanation of Sellers attitude and his unquestioned basketball IQ was simple. "He wanted to rip your heart out."

This is the story of a group of overachievers driving home a spectacular point to the non-believers. Their biggest weapon was that they were rare selfless athletes willing to put ego aside. Read this book and share their delightful journey. I covered the two games they lost at the end. I know that fairy tales don't come true. But as I reread it, I found myself silently rooting for history to somehow magically change the ending. Jeff Kleinbaum lived it as a player and, with the help of Tom Luicci, told a perfect story of a team that was perfect until the final weekend of the season.

INTRODUCTION

THE HEADLINES KEPT COMING ALL year: "Rutgers Beats Purdue," "Rutgers Outlasts St. John's," "Copeland MVP; OK with Phil," "Rutgers set to run UConn out of NCAA," "Sellers Named All-American," "A Reason for Mayhem," "Rutgers Perfect (26–0) Season," "Depth Sends Rutgers to Heights." The 1975–76 Scarlet Knights were a phenomenon, and everyone wanted to be a part of it. Newspapers, radio stations, magazines—all wanted to feature Rutgers's men's basketball team in one form or another. And why not? We won games with quickness, defense, superior athleticism—and we had fun too.

We were only the nineteenth basketball team in NCAA history to go undefeated in the regular season (Indiana would become No. 20 a few nights later); we averaged 93.3 points a game (98.7 during our ten-game home schedule); and there was no shot clock, no dunking, and no three-point line. Our gym was packed beyond capacity; we couldn't walk around campus without talking to people about the season. It was a glorious time to go to Rutgers, and people still remember it with tremendous fondness.

I have been asked many questions about that team over the past fifty years. When people learn I played for Rutgers at that time, they search their memories to uncover interesting tidbits about the players or specific games they remember. Two questions come up the most: Was Phil Sellers as mean as he looked on TV or when they saw him at games? And do I believe the team could be as successful today as it was in the 1970s?

To answer the first question, I explain that Phil's "scowl," as it was called, was probably due to being raised in very difficult conditions in the Bedford Stuyvesant section of Brooklyn, where the crime rate was very high and basketball games were played for very serious stakes. Phil had to be tough, and his persona was just that. I also say that Phil was an off-the-charts competitor, and his game face reflected his focus and intensity. Off the court, he never showed that scowl; he was kind-hearted, friendly, and easygoing.

The second question took a lot of thought. I know that nobody meant any disrespect by it, but I sensed that many people believed we played in an era when the game was slower and more mechanical. When they look at players from that era today, they see men with gray or bald heads, puffy bellies, and a few prominent wrinkles on their faces. *How could you guys have ever been that good?* they think.

After pondering that for a good many years, I finally decided to say exactly what I thought. The 1975–76 Rutgers basketball team would not only compete well against today's athletes but be extremely successful in competing for national championships! I am not suggesting we would go undefeated during the regular season or go to the Final Four with anything close to a 31–0 record. Doing that again would be almost impossible. Even if our team had stayed together for one more year and played the exact same schedule, we probably would not have gone undefeated. There were too many variables to consider, including some luck, and, yes, some calls that needed to go our way.

Our team was a collection of unique individuals who came together as one. We were exceptionally quick and pressed with purpose just about all game, every game. When our opponents somehow got into their offense, we played a team-oriented man-to-man defense that prevented them from feeling comfortable with the ball. Our offense fit our talent to a tee, and if you think the offenses back then wouldn't work in today's game, ask Bruce Pearl of Auburn. His team was ranked No. 1 in the country and playing in the 2025 Final Four as this book was being written. Pearl was a disciple of Dr. Tom Davis of Boston College, who was a disciple of our coach, Tom Young. The offense that

Pearl uses today is the exact same one Coach Young used when we went to the Final Four.

Those who say our team couldn't compete as well today as some of the others should study tapes of us and listen to people who saw us play on a regular basis. We had a motto that I think others should follow. That motto was best described by Bruce Scherer, my teammate. He said, "First is first, and second is last." We trusted each other and always had each other's back. Nobody ever slouched in games, and perhaps more importantly, during practice.

The team was made up of special parts too. Phil Sellers was a first-team All-American; he is still Rutgers's all-time leading scorer and re-bounder. All great teams need go-to players, and Phil Sellers was ours. Mike Dabney was a New Jersey high jump champion in high school, and he ran as fast or faster than anybody in today's game. He could handle the ball, shoot it well, and play defense with reckless abandon.

Eddie Jordan, our point guard, not only was one of the quickest guards in all of college basketball (hence the nickname Fast Eddie), but he went on to have a nine-year NBA career and twice led the league in steals. Jordan ran our offense like it was an extension of his hands. Did he know the game? His knowledge was so strong that he was hired by the Sacramento Kings, Washington Wizards, and Philadelphia 76ers to be their head coach. He also was the head coach of our own Scarlet Knights from 2013–16.

Hollis Copeland, another New Jersey high jump champion, was as athletic a player as any in college basketball. After graduating from Rutgers in 1978, he went on to play for the New York Knicks, who had Patrick Ewing, a top-fifty all-time NBA player. Ewing once said that Hollis was the toughest person he ever went against in practice.

Then there was James Bailey, who three years after the Final Four was picked sixth in the NBA draft. In my opinion, if Bailey could have played for the current Rutgers team, with its superstars Dylan Harper and Ace Bailey, they would not only have made the NCAA tournament but would have been serious contenders to advance far in their bracket.

The bench players were no slouches either. Steve Hefele, Abdel Anderson, and Bruce Scherer could shoot the ball with anybody, and they did it by creating their own shots. Mark Conlin and Stan Nance were great ballhandlers who knew how to get the ball to their teammates in open spots and could score themselves. Mike Palko and I were what coaches called "grit players." We would do anything to contribute, as Mike did fabulously when he was replaced in the starting lineup by Bailey. Mike not only accepted his new role graciously, but he went out of his way to help with Bailey's progress. Winning was not the important thing for all of us—it was the only thing, and we did it exactly as we were taught.

You've heard my views on this question, so I decided that I would ask some people who know college basketball extremely well. Dick Vitale, who coached at Rutgers, the University of Detroit, and the Detroit Pistons before embarking on a Hall of Fame career at ESPN; Bill Raftery, who was head coach at Seton Hall University when we played them and then also went on to a Hall of Fame broadcasting career at CBS sports; and, finally, my teammate Eddie Jordan, who played nine years in the NBA and went on to be head coach of the Philadelphia 76ers, Washington Wizards, and Sacramento Kings.

Dick Vitale was very cooperative and happy to contribute his views. Here is what he said when I asked him how good the 1976 Rutgers team would be today: "Rutgers could have absolutely played in today's game. They had the skill and the quickness to do it. They also were as athletic as any of the great teams now."

Bill Raftery had a similar assessment: "Yes, of course that Rutgers team could have been successful in today's game. They had quickness that translates to today's game, they were multitalented, with several pros, and they had an inside protector (James Bailey)."

Finally, Eddie Jordan: "I'm convinced that our '76 team could have been very successful in today's era because we had superb athleticism, quickness, and speed at every position, one-to-twelve. Our quickness allowed us to press full court effectively, defend in the half court, and rebound with teams much bigger than us."

College basketball on the East Coast was starved for national attention at the time and looking for a team to lead it. Yes, in 1965, the East Coast had the Princeton Tigers, led by eventual New York Knick and

New Jersey senator Bill Bradley, who was superb that year and took them to the Final Four. Then there were the 1971 Fordham Rams, led by their Hall of Fame coach, Digger Phelps. Their 22–3 record caught the imagination of New York City, and they were great for college basketball. But Princeton and Fordham were clearly the exceptions, not the rule. In 1976, our team at Rutgers changed all of that.

I hope you will enjoy this story of our team. It will take you through the same journey we took before, during, and after the 1975–76 season. You will follow each player's recruitment and meet the guys who went on to have remarkable basketball careers. You will get the inside account of what it was like to play in "the Barn," where the seating capacity was 2,800, but it sounded more like 28,000. If you were a follower of Rutgers basketball back then, you must have heard about the paint chips falling from the ceiling when the crowd erupted, which was very often.

Any discussion about the Rutgers basketball team in the 1970s wouldn't be complete without including the political and social climate that existed then. On the Rutgers campus, in New Jersey, and throughout the US, the atmosphere was charged with issues relating to race, women's rights, and war, which were in the forefront of the news at that time. Our team found itself in the middle of that debate and actually became much closer as a unit because of it.

In this book, I will recap our greatest triumphs and our near-upset losses. You will follow the team through the regular season, the Eastern College Athletic Conference (ECAC) championships in Madison Square Garden, the last-second win in Providence, Rhode Island, the Eastern Regionals in Greensboro, North Carolina, and, finally, the Final Four in Philadelphia. You will hear from the players, coaches, and our opponents as they express their views on the team before and after those games.

No book like this would be complete without hearing from the fans. I've devoted a chapter to them in which they share their memories with fans everywhere. I spoke with many people who wrote about their memories, and it was a fantastic experience to hear about those times through their own words.

Finally, you will go behind the scenes with us as we traveled the country, representing our school, our state, and the fans we loved so much. You will see a side of the characters of this great story that very few people know.

I knew that writing this book would take me back in time. My concern was that my teammates' memories might have faded and important parts of our story would be lost forever. I shouldn't have worried though. Each player remembered each and every game and added incredible insight as I chronicled this special team. Enjoy the book.

WAIT UNTIL NEXT YEAR

Denny Crum only needed to see us for forty minutes in March of 1975 to know we had something special going on with our basketball program.

We played in the National Invitation Tournament (NIT) my first two years at Rutgers; at the time, college basketball was just starting to shift its focus to the NCAA tournament, pressuring its best teams to play there instead of the NIT. But in 1975 we made the NCAA tournament for the first time in school history.

There was no league in the East for schools like Rutgers back then—just as there was no shot clock, no three-point shot, and no dunking allowed—so we had to win a two-game qualification event in the ECAC Tournament at Madison Square Garden to make the thirty-two-team NCAA tournament field.

We did that by handling St. Peter's and then holding off St. John's, 79–77, at a raucous Madison Square Garden that was split equally among Rutgers and St. John's fans. The Garden was St. John's second home, but it was our home away from home as well, since we played there so often. It wasn't unusual to see packed trains leaving New Brunswick and heading for Penn Station and Madison Square Garden when we played in New York City.

Our Midwest Regional draw in the 1975 NCAA tournament was Louisville, a powerhouse team coached by Crum, a future Hall of Famer and future two-time national champion.

We played about as well as we could in the first half, taking a 46–44 halftime lead with Phil Sellers, Mike Dabney, and Eddie Jordan leading the way. But Louisville had more postseason experience and an All-American in Junior Bridgeman, who scored a career-high thirty-six points as the Cardinals pulled away late for a 91–78 win.

The final margin was misleading, and Crum knew it. We forced twenty-three turnovers and played a terrific first thirty minutes in our NCAA debut.

Afterward, Crum was effusive in his praise of our team, noting that we were "exceptionally quick" and that we had a chance to do something special the next season, because the nucleus of our team was underclassmen.

He was spot on with that. (By the way, I went 2-for-2 for four points in the game, although one of my baskets came when I overthrew a lob pass that went into the basket.)

Crum wasn't alone in his assessment that we were poised for bigger and better things in the 1975–76 season.

Assistant Coach John McFadden, the lone holdover from Dick Lloyd's staff, pointed to a 96–82 win at LaSalle during the 1974–75 season as a telling result. In that game, Bruce Scherer came off the bench and shut down LaSalle's great player, Joe "Jellybean" Bryant, who would become the father of NBA legend Kobe Bryant. The LaSalle Explorers were ranked No. 17 in the Associated Press Top 20 basketball poll at the time.

"We knew the year before that we would be good the next year," said McFadden, a Philadelphia native. "That year (1974–75), we played at LaSalle, and we were down fourteen at the half. I can still remember it was 42–28, because that's my hometown. And we came out and scored twenty-eight straight points. You do something like that, and you don't forget it.

"So, the following year, we knew we had a really good mix. I remember walking into a pharmacy near my parents' house and getting *Sports Illustrated*, and they had us ranked seventh or eighth. We knew we were going to be good. How good? By ten or twelve games into the season, we knew we had something special going on. This was not the

Rutgers that played Lafayette, Lehigh, and Colgate. This was a whole different animal."

As a team, we felt something special awaited us that year.

"I looked at our schedule before the season and I remember thinking, 'I don't see us losing more than one game,' and that game was probably going to be in the Poinsettia Classic, because I knew nothing about the teams in it," said star guard Mike Dabney. "As far as the rest of the schedule, I thought we could run through it, because we had a lot of returning talent and tremendous chemistry.

"What I didn't know was how good James Bailey was going to be," he said about the freshman center. "His impact made a big difference."

But it really wasn't until off-season decisions by Sellers and Dabney that the optimism for 1975–76 became valid.

"Phil and I actually explored going hardship (in the NBA draft) after our junior seasons (1974–75)," said Dabney. "We explored it to test the waters. We really couldn't get a definitive answer as to where either one of us would go in the draft. There were rumors about the old ABA not surviving much longer. That was one of the reasons we took a look at that." (The American Basketball Association was formed in 1967 to rival the NBA. In 1976, the leagues merged, with four ABA teams—the Nuggets, Pacers, Spurs, and Nets—joining the senior league.)

Secured in the knowledge that his two best players would return as seniors, Head Coach Tom Young entered the 1975–76 season with heightened expectations—but he kept his optimism reasonable.

"We had a good year the year before," Young told the Scarlet Spotlight podcast years later. "Not just myself, but we all felt we would be pretty good with the experience we got and the discipline we got into the guys, and they accepted it really well.

"So going into the season we felt good about it. But there were no thoughts about the Final Four or about going undefeated."

But by game five, other coaches were starting to recognize that something special was afoot.

"We played Penn (a 95–80 win), and (coach) Chuck Daly said after the game, 'This team could go undefeated,'" said Young. "I said, 'Thanks a lot, Chuck.'"

"Fortunately, we dodged all the close games and ended up (in the Final Four), which was probably a shock to most people in the basketball world."

DESTINATION NEW BRUNSWICK

R UTGERS WAS NOT A TOP-TIER basketball school in the late 1960s and early 1970s. The national media did not report their scores on a day-to-day basis, and most players who had aspirations of going pro didn't think to come to New Brunswick, New Jersey. Then, in 1972, things changed dramatically. And when I accepted one of five scholarships offered by Dick Lloyd and his staff, I did not realize that I was almost the cause of Phil Sellers, Rutgers's eventual all-time leading scorer and rebounder, not coming to the school.

I'd better explain. I was part of the first recruiting class at Rutgers to receive basketball scholarships. Prior to my freshman year, 1972–73, the school awarded athletic scholarships based only on financial need. That changed in 1972, when the school approved five basketball scholarships for Head Coach Dick Lloyd to hand out.

After visiting St. John's—just two miles from my house in Queens, New York—as well as Rhode Island, Virginia, and Tulane, and then turning down an offer from the New York Mets, who drafted me in June of 1972, I made the decision to attend Rutgers.

I became Coach Loyd's fifth and final recruit that year, joining Mike Dabney, Bruce Scherer, Mike Palko, and Ronny Williams (he left after one year). Sellers had already determined he was going to Notre Dame.

But when Sellers changed his mind late in the process and decided to come to Rutgers, Lloyd and his staff found themselves scrambling to find another scholarship.

"We made five offers to players, and Phil Sellers—who we wanted to give one of the scholarships to—turned us down," Lloyd remembers vividly. "Then we got word in the spring that Phil wasn't comfortable going to Notre Dame and he called (Rutgers's then–Assistant Coach) Dick Vitale to tell him he had changed his mind and wanted to come to Rutgers.

"The problem was, we only had those five scholarships. So when Sellers originally turned us down, we gave the last scholarship to Jeff Kleinbaum. So I went to athletic director, Al Twitchell, and explained the situation to him. Al went to an alumnus named Herb Goodkind, who had funded scholarships in the past, and told him we needed another scholarship, but we didn't have any money left because we were budgeted for five scholarships and we gave them all out. We asked Herb if he would fund a sixth scholarship for that one year. Fortunately for us, he did. That was the scholarship that went to Phil Sellers."

So, thank you, Herb Goodkind. I can't imagine carrying around the burden for life of being the guy who prevented Phil Sellers from attending Rutgers.

In my case, I had five scholarship offers to consider. All of my other teammates had multiple offers as well—Mike Dabney originally committed to Dayton and Eddie Jordan committed to Loyola of Chicago—before deciding on Rutgers.

Dabney was one of the top players in New Jersey during his senior year at East Orange High School, and his team won a state championship, so prying him away from Dayton was a coup.

"I was set to go to Dayton," said Dabney, who is fourth on the school's career scoring list with 1,902 points. "They recruited me pretty heavily. When I went out to visit, I played in an All-American game there. I remember they had a tartan floor that made you feel like you could jump out of the gym. Plus, they played the Kentuckys and UCLAs of the world.

"It just came down to Dick Vitale constantly coming to my games and writing me letters all of the time. I had never even watched a Rutgers game before I decided to go there. It was because Dick Vitale was relentless in recruiting me."

Jordan's decision to come to Rutgers was more a case of fortuitous timing. The eventual four-year point guard from Washington, DC— who had never been a true point guard before—had signed a letter of intent to play for Loyola of Chicago.

"Maybe a week after I signed with Loyola, Tom Young got the job at Rutgers," said Jordan. "Tom had recruited me when he was at American University. He invited me to come to the American University basketball banquet and told me to bring a date. I brought my mother. At the end of the night, he told me I was the only prospect who had ever brought his mother as a date.

"He said, 'I really want you to come to American University.' But I didn't want to. I wanted to try something outside of Washington. So I signed with Loyola. When Tom Young got the job at Rutgers, he convinced me to come on a visit. Phil Sellers took me on my visit and, to be honest, I thought Rutgers was only Douglass College, because that's mostly what I saw of the campus. The reason Phil only took me there was because Douglass was an all-female school, and he thought I would like that. At the end of the weekend, that Sunday morning, I decided I wanted to go to Rutgers. I knew they had a really good class of sophomores at the time and that Phil Sellers was one of the best players in the country. So I knew there was the nucleus of something special."

Jordan finished his career with 1,632 points and remains the school's leader in assists with 585.

James Bailey is often referred to as "the missing piece" for our Final Four run. His size, rebounding, and shot blocking proved to be the perfect complement to a team that needed exactly that. When he became the starter in the sixth game that year, it gave us a starting lineup that consisted of a freshman (Bailey), a sophomore (Hollis Copeland), a junior (Jordan), and two seniors (Sellers and Dabney).

It also gave us a lineup that should have been sponsored by Amtrak, the passenger train company, with Bailey from Boston, Copeland from

Trenton, Jordan from Washington, Sellers from Brooklyn, and Dabney from East Orange.

But it took some deception to get the thoughtful and quiet-spoken Bailey to get on board as part of the roster.

"I was fortunate enough to be a good student, so graduating from Xaverian Brothers High School (in Boston), I knew I could get into any of the schools that were recruiting me," said Bailey. "What the coaches didn't understand back then is I wasn't this overly minded basketball guy. I didn't wake up every day saying I wanted to go pro. My whole thing was I wanted to go to a school where they were going to take care of me and pay for my education, so I could get a degree for free. That was my whole objective. So I visited a couple of different schools.

"I visited some schools that made it very tempting for me. I had two universities that were willing to let me bring my best friend with me.

"The biggest lure to Rutgers was the attention and the national recognition the school had academically. But the main reason—and I mean this with all due respect to Tom Young—was (Assistant Coach) Joe Boylan. Joe Boylan was at my house every other day, and I'm talking about coming to a hardcore inner-city environment. You can talk about the Bronx and Harlem and Brooklyn, where Phil Sellers was from, but if you know your history about Roxbury, it is right up there with any of those places.

"Joe was at my house constantly. In fact, I have to say at least 25 percent of the time I thought he was watching me at practice, but he really wasn't there. I would be on the practice floor, and he would be up in the rafters, and I would wave to him and he would wave back, so I knew Joe was in the stands. After practices and games, he would never stay because he had to rush back to New Jersey.

"Little did I know—and I found this out afterward—some of those times it was Joe's brother in the stands watching me. He and his brother could pass for twins, so you would swear that it was Joe Boylan when you looked up in the stands."

That was enough to lure a player who is third all-time on Rutgers's career scoring list with 2,032 points and is second on the program's career rebounding list.

Hollis Copeland starred in basketball and track at Ewing High School in Trenton, NJ, which he said led to an estimated "two hundred scholarship offers between basketball and track."

"More so for basketball than track," he said. "My junior year, I was the state high jump champion in New Jersey. Mike Dabney was a high jump champion in high school too, but during an earlier year.

"There were some schools that were willing to let me do both sports. Frank Gagliano was the track coach at Rutgers back then. So my freshman and sophomore years, I was with the track team after basketball. My freshman year, Tom Young let me run track for the full season. After that, with my scholarship being for basketball, we came to an agreement for my sophomore year that he would let me compete in a few meets but not for the entire season. My sophomore year I went right from the Final Four to track practice.

"Coach Young cut out track entirely after my sophomore year."

I had a similar situation after the Final Four. The Final Four was on a Monday, and Wednesday we played Columbia in baseball. Not practice. It was a game. I got to the field and the coach (Matt Bolger) says, "You're in the starting lineup." I had not picked up a baseball for almost six months. (Hopefully, no one digs up a box score to remind people of how my at-bats went that day.)

The rest of our roster arrived at Rutgers in a fairly conventional manner, although Abdel Anderson first signed with Manhattan College.

"I wasn't really crazy about the social life there," said Anderson. "So I went back and reconsidered my options. It was going to be Manhattan College, Boston College, Fordham, or Rutgers. When I visited Rutgers, I fell in love with the place. I felt so at home. Rutgers had a lot of things going for it. The previous year they played exceptionally well against Louisville in the NCAA tournament, and Rutgers wasn't that far from home (Belleville, New Jersey). I told them at Manhattan College what I was doing, and they let me out of my letter of intent. So it worked out."

Mark Conlin thought he was headed to Boston College, "but BC decided to take someone else, and that left me out in the cold.

"Howard Garfinkel (Five-Star Basketball Camp founder) recommended me to Tom Young, who eventually came to my house and offered me a scholarship. Before I said yes, I asked him if we were going to play Boston College any time in the next few years, and when he told me yes, I told him, 'I am coming to Rutgers.'"

Fast forward to the 1975–76 season. Game three happened to be at Boston College.

"We crushed them (105–82), and I had a good game," Conlin said. "After the game, when we were shaking hands with their team, I shook hands with their head coach (Bob Zuffelato) and told him, 'You messed up, Coach. You should have taken me when you had the chance.'"

Steve Hefele had narrowed his choices to Rutgers, St. John's, and Massachusetts before eventually committing to Tom Young.

"When I visited and went to a game, they looked pretty strong," Hefele said. "And they had a lot of guys coming back, so I knew they were building something good. I enjoyed my visit, and the coaches made me feel wanted. It was just a comfortable feel."

In my six-player class, which included two of the best players in program history, Sellers and Dabney, the one who actually got things rolling was Bruce Scherer. He holds the distinction of being the first player at Rutgers to receive a full basketball scholarship.

"I decided to sign early because I didn't want to go through the whole travel thing and recruiting visits my senior year of high school," Scherer said. "I visited Tennessee. I did not like the environment there. St. Joseph's, LaSalle, and Lafayette were options, but I chose Rutgers because of the environment.

"Then, of course, I liked Coach Lloyd and Assistant Coach Vitale and the people around the program. I just felt comfortable there immediately with the environment and the type of people in the basketball program.

"When I got there, the talent was obvious right away."

Mike Palko, a senior who started the first five games at center during the Final Four run before being replaced by Bailey, had narrowed his choices out of high school to Rutgers and Princeton.

"Coach Pete Carril came to a lot of my games, as did the Rutgers staff," said Palko. "What I think sold me on Rutgers was that they were trying to create a new chapter in the athletic program with the offering of full NCAA scholarships, whereas Princeton was based on financial need or academic standing. The enthusiasm around Rutgers basketball then tilted it toward Rutgers for me. I really liked Dick Lloyd and Dick Vitale, and I liked the direction they were headed in. It was an exciting opportunity. I think it was the launching of a new era of Rutgers athletics."

Or, as Rutgers's then-president, Edward Bloustein, announced at the time: Rutgers was not just going big-time. It was going "bigger time."

Stan Nance, a late summer signee, had come from a basketball family. His younger brother, Greg Nance, was a solid three-year starter for West Virginia, and his older brother, Reggie Nance, was elected to the University of Maryland at Baltimore County Sports Hall of Fame following his basketball career.

Following an excellent career at Spingarn High School in Washington, DC, Nance was recruited by Tom Young at American University and followed Young to Rutgers. He did not sign his letter of intent until July.

The Sellers recruiting story is well known by now. Dick Vitale put a full-court press on him, but he wound up signing with Notre Dame.

"My basic sales pitch was, 'We've never had one like you,'" said Vitale. "I told him, 'All of those other schools recruiting you have had a Phil Sellers. But we've never had one like you.' I kept pounding that point home because I believed it.

"I could tell he had a tough time telling me on the phone that he was going to Notre Dame. I wished him luck and told him that Notre Dame was a great program and a great school."

Sellers would later concede that he was concerned about fitting in academically at Notre Dame.

"I think that had a lot to do with me changing my mind," he said.

Rutgers was not party to the National Letter of Intent (a legal commitment), so he was not committed, and it was not a problem when Sellers backed out of his Notre Dame commitment to sign with Rutgers.

All that was left was for Rutgers to find a scholarship for him. Thanks to Herb Goodkind, it did.

THE BARN

THERE WAS NO COLLEGE BASKETBALL environment quite like the Barn (a.k.a. the College Avenue Gym). Opened in 1932 on the site where Rutgers and Princeton played the first college football game in 1869, the Barn seated between 2,800 and 3,200 on game days, depending on the fire marshal's mood.

It really wasn't much bigger than a high school gym. There was seating on three sides, and the scorer's table and players' benches were situated in front of a wall that ran the length of the gym and proclaimed in big, bold letters: KNIGHT COUNTRY.

When that giant wall slid open, you could see the swimming pool. But you knew it was there before you ever saw it, because of the strong chlorine smell. When the crowd got really loud and rowdy, paint chips would flutter from the ceiling, causing a stoppage in play so the court could be swept. Every game it seemed the fans were determined to cause those paint chips to fall with the noise level they created.

I think it's safe to say that no other eventual Final Four team has ever played in a building quite like the Barn.

The first time I walked into the building was as a recruit. I was invited with my parents to a game, and when we walked in, the entire scene was surreal.

I had been to many gyms and arenas in my life, but I had never experienced anything quite like the Barn. The first thing I noticed was the separating wall behind the benches. I had never seen anything like that in a basketball arena. It wasn't until later that I learned its purpose.

The game-day atmosphere eventually erased any doubts or concerns about the Barn as a home-court advantage.

"It was a very hard place to play," said Bill Raftery, of Seton Hall. "The impact of the fans was about like your high school days, when you inbound the ball and the fans were right there, and they could actually grab hold of you."

Raftery's Pirates gave up 119 points when they played at the Barn that year. That's a Rutgers record for points that still stands.

"I loved playing at the Barn," said Mike Dabney. "The adrenaline rush you got from a packed place, the sound reverberating off the walls, made it seem like there were 5,000 or 6,000 people there. And the fans were so close—they were right on top of you.

"I remember one time there was a turnover, and we got the ball, and I was taking it out on the baseline under the opponent's basket, and I leaned over to some fans, and I said, 'Watch this.' Phil and I had made eye contact, and sure enough I threw a baseball pass, and Phil went in for a layup on the other side of the court."

During that 1975–76 season, there was never an empty seat at our games. You almost had to know someone to get a ticket, and the demand for a seat was off the charts because we only played ten home games that year.

Stan Nance figured out how to take advantage of the overwhelming demand too.

"I loved playing at the Barn, and for the style of play we had, it was the perfect place for us," he said. "We were pressing you from the time you got off the bus, and to have the fans on three-quarters of the sides of the gym right on top of you, I thought that was a big advantage for us."

He continued, "The gym was not big at all. Obviously, I figured out that my four comp tickets were worth a lot of money. And Stan Nance got paid. I didn't give my tickets to other students. Instead, I made some money from those tickets. That was a sweet deal."

Game day was always a special experience, no matter who we were playing. It started with our pregame meal, which we ate at George

Mackaronis's Town House Restaurant across the street from the New Brunswick train station.

Mr. Mac was a legend in Rutgers basketball circles. A captain of the basketball team during his senior year at Rutgers, he founded the Court Club and was its president for thirty years. More importantly, he was a terrific man who absolutely adored anything Rutgers and treated each player as if he were one of his sons.

Game-day meal was not a set menu. We could eat anything we wanted. Mark Conlin usually aggravated me because he would always order a steak so rare that when it was served, he said he wanted to able "to hear it moo."

Eddie Jordan liked to have London broil, potatoes, and vegetables (why I remember that so vividly, I'm not quite sure). For a lightning-quick point guard, I always marveled at how much he ate. He was a beast at the dinner table.

After the meal, Bruce Scherer and I would go back to our apartment on Easton Avenue and relax for a while. Then we would go to the gym early, which was our habit for everything we did, and get ready to play. As soon as we got there, the lure of the Barn took over. We would go down the back stairs to the old locker room, which was nothing more than a separate room with high school-style lockers with our names over them. It was nothing like the luxurious facilities players have today.

We had no amenities. We just had a cramped bare-bones locker room and the unmistakable scent of chlorine.

Once dressed, each player would prepare in his own way. Coach Young would then come in, go over the game plan, and remind us what we were playing for. In the Final Four year, he didn't have to say much in that regard, but I was always amazed how ready we always were when we left that locker room.

We would then walk up those same back stairs we came down earlier and huddle just inside the door before we went through it to go into the gym. Those few seconds before we ran out were something I will remember for the rest of my life.

I was third in line behind Eddie Jordan, who led us out, and Mark Conlin, who followed him. You could hear the loud crowd noise before we ever stepped on the court, because they were usually lustily booing our opponent, who took the floor just before we did. Eddie then would turn back to everyone and announce, "Ready, guys?" And out we went.

The adrenaline rush was incredible as we entered. The band played the Rutgers fight song, and the ground actually started to shake a bit as the crowd got into it. I can't describe how ready that music and that crowd made us feel.

"Our pregame entrance triggered deafening cheers and the absolute best chorus of the Rutgers fight song," said Mike Palko. "Just a great adrenaline rush. The crowd knew it was fueling us, and us them. It was a mutually beneficial experience."

Palko continued: "When we started our layup line after we ran a drill we called 'single exchange,' I felt I could jump through the gym. I often wondered what the other team was going through when all this was happening. I was just glad I was a Rutgers player."

During home games, the crowd was into it from the very beginning, working itself into a frenzy after our first basket. Then the paint chips would start falling and the atmosphere gave us the best home-court advantage in college basketball.

"I loved it, because I knew what to expect," said Hollis Copeland. "The smell of chlorine from the pool, the paint chips falling from the ceiling, the fans right on top of you. We loved it there. The opposition didn't know what was happening.

"Think about it. You come into our gym after you've heard about this Rutgers team. So you're focusing on the team. Then you go into the gym, and you sit down on your bench and you're like, 'What is that smell? Where is it coming from?' There was a partition there that blocked off the pool behind it.

"Then you see the fans coming in during warm-ups, and all of a sudden, the gym starts shrinking. We would start playing and running, and the fans were into it, and all of a sudden you see the dandruff coming down from the ceiling out of nowhere.

"You almost think the place is possessed. You have to play under these conditions for the first time. We're used to it. Before they knew it, we're up by ten or fifteen points, and they couldn't wait to get out of the building."

Abdel Anderson, a freshman during the Final Four season, looked a bit starry-eyed when he ran out with the team the first time of his home career. "Running through the side door into the gym was incredible. The student seats were made out of wood and metal and when the crowd got into it by stomping their feet in unison, as they did when we came out, the floor actually shook."

During that 1975–76 season we averaged 98.8 points per game for our ten home games and hit 100 points five times. Our average margin of victory at home that year was twenty points.

The Barn was unique and gave us a considerable advantage on game days.

"For some of us, it was a short walk through the quad and campus to the Barn," said Steve Hefele. "Just the familiarity of the dorms, library, and classrooms as you crossed College Avenue to enter the gym was very comforting. Then, descending the stairs to the locker room and hearing the familiar sounds from the stereo gave you a "Yeah, let's do this" vibe of things to come.

"Then we'd slowly start getting dressed, and the bantering back and forth with teammates before heading off to the trainer's room to get taped set the tone for the upcoming game. There was always that confidence in knowing the level of support that you would feel from the proximity and noise of the crowd. Its effect on your opponent was another huge advantage."

Once Coach Young finished his review of the game plan and his pep talk, the adrenaline started to kick in as we all anticipated the roar of the crowd and the energy of the pep band. What a tremendous boost as we took the floor. It was a natural high for sure. It was often difficult to hear any of the visiting crowd, as they were easily drowned out by our raucous supporters. During the games the decibel level at times drowned out anything Coach Young was attempting to communicate. When the crescendo reached a level when the paint chips on the old ceiling fell to the gym floor and the game was delayed to sweep them up, it made us feel invincible.

"There were other small gyms back then lovingly known as pits, dungeons, or cages that were difficult to play in," said Hefele. "But the Barn ranked right up there with any of them. I got to play my senior year in the newly constructed Rutgers Athletic Center. Although it was a big step up for the program, and one that needed to happen, to me there really was no comparison to the atmosphere experienced in the Barn."

Today, whenever I go to New Brunswick for any reason, I make it a point to visit the Barn. I park in the back and walk through the same doors I went through going to games fifty years ago. I stop at the door where we ran out, and I look over the scene there today. I still see the people standing and cheering rhythmically. When I go into the gym today, it looks exactly as it did then. The chairs are red, the wall is in place with the pool behind it, and the scoreboard is the same one used back in the 1970s. It's a great reminder of one of the best times of my life.

THE TUMULTUOUS '70S

THERE WAS SO MUCH SPILLOVER from the turbulent 1960s into our college years in the early to mid-'70s that it was almost impossible to ignore the dynamic social shift taking place. The civil rights movement was in its early stages; the Vietnam War was still raging (and sparking the anti-war protests that divided the country); women were fighting for equal rights; Watergate left an ugly stain on the White House; there were gas shortages (remember the long lines just to fill up?); and environmental causes moved into the collective consciousness of the younger generation.

It wasn't until 1972 that the first class of women was admitted to Rutgers College (Rutgers University was divided into five campuses then: Rutgers College, Cook College, Livingston College, Douglass College, and Busch). Four hundred seventy women were admitted, as well as seventy-five transfers, compared to almost seven thousand men.

Those social issues became an unavoidable part of the storyline for my class, which included Phil Sellers, Mike Dabney, Mike Palko, and Bruce Scherer.

And that's the environment that we as eighteen-year-old kids entered into. Every player on our team brought with them to New Brunswick, NJ, their vastly different experiences growing up in two of the most consequential decades in American history. Phil Sellers came from Bedford Stuyvesant, a low-income, inner-city section of Brooklyn, NY known for many things, including a high crime rate. Mike Dabney grew up in East Orange, NJ, a city that was once voted the cleanest American city in the US (1964). Five years later, that same city was suffering from regional economic trends and the decline of manufacturing and industrial jobs. White people moved out to the suburbs and in 1967, the Newark riots played a devastating role in many of the northeast cities in America, including EO. By 1972, when Mike arrived, East Orange High School was 90 percent Black and its team was 100 percent Black.

Bellville, New Jersey, where Abdel Anderson grew up, was a middle-class, mostly Italian community, and the high school reflected that. Most of the school was White (65 percent), and the community was stable with two-parent homes.

Eddie Jordan came from a private Catholic college-prep school that was well regarded for its academics, diversity and commitment to social justice (Archbishop Carroll High School). The school was 75 percent Black (25 percent White) and the team was 85 percent Black. Eddie claims that there were no racial issues in the town, the school, or the team to speak of.

JB grew up in Roxbury, Massachusetts, an inner-city neighborhood of Boston, which he described as "hard core." He traveled every day over ninety minutes to Xaverian Brothers High School in Westwood, MA, where the student body had 850 young people and only five of them were Black. Xaverian was recognized as the number one Catholic high school in the entire state at that time.

Hollis Copeland, from Ewing, New Jersey, moved there from nearby Trenton when he was ten years old. Ewing High School, the town's public school, was predominately White (65 percent), but had a significant African American presence in its student body. The community was considered middle class at that time. He commented for this book that he really didn't face a great deal of racial conflict growing up.

Mark Conlin and I came from Queens, New York. Mark went to Bishop Reilly High School, and came from an Irish Catholic section of Douglaston, while I went to Martin Van Buren High School, a very large public school (5,500 students) which was about 70 percent White.

The community I grew up in, Bayside, was predominantly middle class and had a large Jewish population.

Bruce Scherer and Mike Palko came from Morris and Warren counties (NJ) respectively. Bruce went to Parsippany Hills High School, which was 98 percent White and middle class, while Mike went to Hackettstown High School. Hackettstown was a blue-collar town, whose families believed strongly in education. Bruce's community was the classic "bedroom community" of New York and the families were mostly two-parent households with many of the adults traveling to New York for "professional" jobs.

Steve Hefele and Stan Nance came from pretty different backgrounds from one another. Steve went to East Rockaway High School out on Long Island, which only had one Black student in the entire school (Hefele's best friend).

Stan Nance went to Spingarn High School in Northeast Washington, DC, which was an inner-city high school. Students either took public transportation or walked to school and the makeup of the high school was 99.8 percent Black and lower class.

What you will soon read was thrown at us during our time on and off the court at Rutgers during this era and my hope is that you you'll agree that we were a very special group of people, who, with the right leadership, stepped up and accomplished remarkable things while learning valuable lessons along the way.

I asked the players recently what it was that contributed to us going from being twelve young athletes with incredibly diverse backgrounds and cultures to such a cohesive group of players who would do anything for each other and grow closer and closer as we got older.

Steve Hefele said, "Basketball has a way of uniting people even when the odds are stacked against you."

Mike Dabney said something similar, "We didn't know each other but we did know that there was a common thread that kept us together. That thread was Rutgers basketball."

Stan Nance pointed to family as to why our team was so close, despite our different backgrounds.

"Most of the people I know were raised the right way. They lived with their moms or grandparents and were taught the difference between right and wrong from day one."

Finally, Hollis Copeland probably put it best: "Winning was the key motivation for our existence."

Looking at all this from the vantage point of time one would have a difficult time believing that these twelve men would have ever associated with one another, never mind work together for a common goal as lofty as ours turned out to be. Under the circumstances we were faced with, our backgrounds simply should not have allowed that. Yet, from the very first day we walked on the practice court of Rutgers University, led by our brilliant coach, Tom Young, and his staff, we did exactly that. There were some wonderful triumphs that our basketball team had in 1975–76. But none were more impressive than the triumph we enjoyed then and now, the triumph of winning games and creating a brotherhood.

On December 4, 1973, in our game against Pittsburgh—the second game of my sophomore year—a group of approximately 100 to 150 predominantly African American students made their way from the stands onto the court during a time-out to protest racism and minority programs at Rutgers, staging a sit-in at midcourt with three minutes left in the first half.

Despite impassioned pleas from Sellers and Dabney over the public address system, the protesters refused to budge. We wound up forfeiting the game as a result.

"I was pretty disappointed with what happened that day," said Dabney. "You have a right to protest, but you protest in the right venue. I didn't think disrupting our basketball game, after we had practiced hours upon hours, was the right way to go about it. I thought it was kind of selfish and something that should have transpired outside our basketball game.

"Phil and I tried to talk to the crowd to convince them to let us continue, but they didn't pay us any attention. I just felt it could have been addressed elsewhere, but I guess they wanted to get the most impact they could."

A lot of my teammates were unsure about what was happening. Eddie Jordan was one of them.

"I was sort of naive to what was going on at the time," Jordan said. "I went to an all-boys, predominantly White Catholic high school. When I got to Rutgers, it was a totally different situation for me culturally, going to school with girls and with people with different backgrounds. Like I said, I was naive at the time.

"We had four Black starters then and I didn't think there was anything unusual about that at the time. Mostly what I remember after the students came down from the stands and sat on the court is Phil Sellers grabbing the public address microphone and pleading with the protesters to let us finish the game. So it was a really strange scene.

"I eventually grew to understand what the reason was for it and all of the issues they were protesting at the time. We were kind of isolated from that as basketball players. I guess I really wasn't up to speed on what was happening at the time."

Even during the greatest basketball season in school history, the issue of race became an inescapable part of the narrative of that year.

When James Bailey, then a freshman, replaced Mike Palko, a senior, in the sixth game of the 1975–76 season, it marked the first time Rutgers would consistently field an all-Black starting five. That lineup remained unchanged for the final twenty-eight games of the season.

In the previous two seasons, Rutgers had sporadically used an all-Black starting five, but not for extended stretches.

"Mike Palko was the absolute best about the situation," said Bailey. "Not one day, not one time, did I ever feel uncomfortable about what happened. In fact, during practices, I probably got just as much support and push to continue to do better as anybody else. There was never an issue. Not one time. Mike was my biggest supporter.

"As far as the fans, it was a rough time. I was aware when I became the starter that we now had an all-Black starting five. But I had experienced that kind of treatment from Boston, because I went to a high school that had eight hundred students—all boys, and only five were Black. When that happened at Rutgers, there were a couple of times when the starting five was announced that Tom Young would have to go on the court and tell the fans to stop throwing stuff. Even though we were winning, that was something they were not ready for yet. It was such a change. You've got to give Tom credit for doing it.

"I was aware of the significance of Rutgers having an all-Black starting five back then. My hat is off to Tom Young for wanting to do something like that. But he knew chemistry and he knew what was best for us, and he knew that we as a group would understand it."

Alan Venook, then the sports coeditor of *The Daily Targum*, the Rutgers student newspaper, said, "I remember at some games thinking that the crowd was segregated."

Palko was an excellent player and a great teammate, and yet he was often left feeling uncomfortable for no reason other than the racial stress of the times.

"I was booed in my sophomore or junior year whenever there was a heightened tension about a lot of the things that were going on that weren't sitting well with Black and minority students," said Palko. "They introduced me in the starting lineup one time, and I got booed, and Mike Dabney came over to me and said, 'Mike, this has nothing to do with you.' I knew what he meant by that. It was part of the bigger issues that some Black and minority students had with the university. But that did not feel too good.

"It was nice that Mike came over to clarify. Still, it is something I do remember. There was always chatter about whether Rutgers was ready for an all-Black starting five back then. That made me question if part of the reason I was in the starting lineup was because I was a White player.

"Fortunately, winning takes care of anything. If we weren't winning, it may have been a different story. I have mentioned this to some of the guys a couple of times, that it was a blessing that we had guys that could have been detrimental to the team, and it was never an issue. All of us had a lot of pride. A lot of guys would have liked to have played more minutes and had a bigger impact on things. But people who understand the sport know that the strength of the team goes all the way down to the twelfth man. If you're not on the same page as everyone else, that can have a big impact. But this team got along very well, all the way up and down the bench. I think all of us knew the whole was more important than the individual."

Mark Conlin often served as a calming sounding board whenever there was a difficult issue within the team.

"When Mike Palko got booed whenever he came into the game because some fans wanted James Bailey in there, I went to Palko and told him to calm down and just play your game," said Conlin. "I also told him that the team respected him and his game. I think it helped him.

"When Bailey got booed by some White fans, I told him that we were making the right move by getting him in there. I said to him, 'Look around, JB. How many six-foot-nine guys who block shots do you see in the room?'"

With his size, shot blocking, and rebounding ability, Bailey really was the difference maker in our Final Four run, and everyone on the team—even Palko—understood that.

It still made for some uncomfortable moments for one of the greatest players in school history during his freshman year.

"What people don't understand is at that time you were dealing with all of the racial components with school and the general student population," said Bailey. "That was an issue. Within the team it wasn't an issue at all. In fact, they made it extremely comfortable for me within the team.

"It wasn't my mindset to say, 'Hey, I want to start.' I had no pressure from anyone about that situation except one individual—Phil Sellers. Every day on the practice floor, Phil would push the issue of me starting. He would say, 'What are you going to do? Are you going to take the spot? We need you to start.' You know how strong-minded Phil was. I got more pressure from him than anyone or anything else.

"The ones that helped me through the pressure part of it were Mike Dabney and Eddie Jordan. Eddie would say, 'It's all right, JB. Just play. Just play.'"

The ironic thing to me is that we had a roster that mirrored the times in terms of appearance. Bruce Scherer, Phil Sellers, Jordan, and Dabney had beards, and Jordan, Stan Nance, and Assistant Coach Art Perry all sported sizable Afros.

That was not a common sight in college basketball then. "As far as our look, I think we reflected the times," Scherer said. "We worked hard, played hard, and had fun doing it the way we did."

Sellers was particularly intimidating to opponents, simply by his appearance. Beside the facial hair that did little to hide his scowl, he was also physically mature and solidly built.

"It was different for that time," Perry recalled of the facial hair and Afros. "Phil was a man out of high school. He looked even older with that beard. I think all of it was intimidating to a degree. Then you added that physicality and athleticism to it. We were able to overwhelm teams because of that."

And, of course, the coaches all wore those garish leisure suits.

"They were in style back then," said Young.

As a high school student at Martin Van Buren High School, I always had a tremendous interest in the civil rights issues of the time. Van Buren was a very large high school with well over five thousand students, many of whom were bused in from Jamaica, Queens, and other predominantly African American areas.

Thanks to a teacher named David Cohen, I developed a passion for current events and history, and I closely followed the headline-making news of the 1960s and '70s with great interest. The 1960s were a turning point in the struggle for American civil rights, building on landmark events and decisions of the 1950s and eventually bleeding into my college years in the 1970s.

The 1960s saw the assassinations of President John F. Kennedy, Malcolm X, Dr. Martin Luther King Jr., Medgar Evers, and Robert Kennedy. The protests in Birmingham, Alabama, the 1963 March on Washington, and Dr. King's iconic "I Have a Dream" speech, along with the Civil Rights Act of 1964 and the Voting Rights Act of 1965, dominated the minds of students and young people.

These movements were further intensified by protests against the Vietnam War, which loomed heavily, particularly for those approaching the draft age. By 1972, I was of draft age, but I was not called because I had a 2-S student deferment.

Additionally, starting with the 1972–73 season, the NCAA finally relented and allowed freshmen to play varsity basketball, a game-changer for the six-player freshman class (Ronny Williams left after one year) that arrived at Rutgers that fall.

I remember the campus was alive with excitement and turmoil when I got there. I was assigned Room 641 in Hardenberg Hall, where I roomed with Brian Perkins from Ramsey, New Jersey. Brian had a basketball background and had once been recruited by Rutgers. From day one, we became fast friends.

Rutgers was not immune to the racial and political tensions of the era. On October 1, 1990, Rutgers University Press reflected on the efforts to diversify the student body, stating: "In the mid-sixties, the university established committees to recruit Black students and add more Black faculty members. These efforts produced only modest results. By 1968, there were still not enough Black students on campus, but there were enough to create a political presence for the first time."

Just four years before Brian and I stepped onto the Rutgers campus in 1972, Black students staged large protests against the university's admissions policies. In response, the Rutgers Board of Governors adopted a controversial policy aimed at increasing Black enrollment from Camden, Newark, and Trenton. The policy lasted only two years and created unintended problems.

Meanwhile, colleges in the West were at the forefront of student-led movements, successfully shutting down campus activities. Rutgers earned the nickname "Berkeley of the East" (*Newsweek*). If you looked at a Rutgers basketball team picture from 1966, every player was White. That wasn't unique to Rutgers—Princeton's 1965 Final Four team, led by Bill Bradley, was also entirely White.

In contrast, our Final Four team had seven African American and five Caucasian players. To us, race made no difference—we were friends and brothers. However, the environment around us was undeniably charged.

The Pittsburgh protest game in my sophomore year was when it hit all of us personally. We had kicked off the Tom Young era with an impressive road win against Colgate. Our home opener was against a

Pittsburgh team led by future All-American Billy Knight, and it marked the first home game for two Rutgers freshmen, Eddie Jordan and Mark Conlin.

Playing in the Barn was always special, but I was especially excited for Eddie and Mark to experience it. The game started poorly for us. Pittsburgh came out strong, and Knight was scoring at will. We were trailing 36–21 with three minutes left in the first half when everything changed.

That's when a surge of students left the stands for that sit-in at half court. This wasn't a small protest—as I said, there were between 100 and 150 people involved, including many White allies.

Despite the pleas over the loudspeakers from Sellers and Dabney, the protesters refused to leave.

Conlin, in particular, was shaken. This was his first home game, and he had never experienced anything like it. Years later, he recalled his reaction: "I was so upset that I went home to Queens that night and told my parents, 'I didn't sign up for that shit.' "

PHIL "THE THRILL" SELLERS

EVERY BASKETBALL-MINDED KID GROWING UP in New York City in the late 1960s and early 1970s knew the name Phil Sellers, even before he set foot on the Rutgers campus in 1972. He was a legend in the schoolyards of New York and on the high school basketball courts of Brooklyn, earning All-American honors at Thomas Jefferson High School while garnering more than 250 college scholarship offers.

Being from New York City myself, I knew all about Sellers when I first met him at Five-Star Basketball Camp in upstate New York. Five-Star was one of the elite camps for up-and-coming, elite basketball players (how I got there is anyone's guess), and the summer I was there (before my junior year in high school) Phil was there as well, having just earned MVP honors in the prestigious Dapper Dan Classic in Pittsburgh.

At the end of the week at Five-Star Camp, its legendary owner, Howie Garfinkel, sponsored an All-Star game. I was put on the same team as Phil and found myself on the court with him late in the second quarter. We went on a three-on-one fast break, and I had the ball in the middle, with Phil on my left and another player on the right. As we came downcourt, I passed the ball to the guy on my right, who went in for an easy layup.

The other team called time-out, and I was feeling pretty good about myself. But as we came off the court to high-fives, Phil came over to me, got in my face, and barked, "Next time, you throw me the ball on a break."

That was my official welcome to the world of Phil Sellers.

There really were two versions of Phil Sellers. On the basketball court he was all business: intense, intimidating, willing to do whatever it took to win. He would never shy from a big moment either.

He was also physically mature, and his constant scowl reminded opposing players he was not there to make friends.

"Phil was a man out of high school," said Assistant Coach Art Perry.

Sellers acknowledged that his intensity went a little too far sometimes.

"I get involved when I'm playing," he once said. "Sometimes I just get carried away."

Off the court we saw the mild-mannered Phil. He interacted easily with the media and fans, made time for kids, and seemed to enjoy a good laugh.

"Off the court, to sportswriters like myself, he was engaging, co-operative even after losses, smiled easily, made us laugh. And he was honest," said former Rutgers basketball beat writer Paul Franklin. "You don't get those qualities from everyone in the business."

But Sellers's intensity and flailing elbows would occasionally cross the line in practice.

"During my very first practice at Rutgers, Phil and I got into it," said Hollis Copeland. "The very first practice. The way we used to practice is we'd run, do drills, and then go into a scrimmage, and they would divide up the teams. Most coaches try to find chemistry within the team. You can have a first and second team, but you also have to have chemistry with players that may not be starting. I think they were trying to figure out my position at first. I'm trying to find my place on the Rutgers team.

"Phil and I bumped heads down low and we're throwing elbows at each other. It got to the point where we got up in each other's face. Coach Art Perry got between us. He says to us: 'You know what? If you guys want to fight, go downstairs and fight.' At the Barn back then, you had to go downstairs to get to the locker room.

"So we go downstairs to the locker room and we kind of look at each other, and he says, 'Man, what do you want to do?' I said to him: 'What do you want to do?' So he says, 'Let's go get something to eat. I didn't feel like practicing anyway.'

"That set the stage for our relationship. We became so close that when he married Jean Edmonson (his first wife), I was his best man."

Bruce Scherer had a run-in with Sellers during one practice that I thought would escalate into something much worse. It never did.

"Phil was a tough guy. We had moments where we'd mix it up in practice and go at it intently," said Scherer. "You'd get fouled by him constantly, sometimes pretty hard. One day Phil was not appreciative of my efforts and kind of came after me, and Coach Young threw him out of practice because of it.

"Afterward, Phil left a note downstairs on the blackboard in the locker room that said, 'This is not over yet.' But nothing ever came of it."

Sellers's no-nonsense approach set the tone for practice and the season. He was just six-foot-four and 195 pounds, but he wound up as Rutgers's career rebounding leader and all-time scorer. That says a lot about his relentless drive as a player.

"I was a little intimidated by Phil," said Abdel Anderson, who was a freshman during the 1975–76 season. "He would tell you what to do, but he would also back it up by the way he practiced and played. You had to elevate yourself because of that. He would not only talk about it, he would do it. He was just special.

"There was something about Phil. I always looked up to him. Partly scared of him, but he got a lot out of me and gave me a lot of confidence. He had trust in me, and that gave me confidence. He was one of those players who was on a whole other level. He was a great defensive player and a tremendous rebounder for someone his height. He was just relentless going after rebounds. He had some kind of competitive heart."

Sellers did not hesitate at times to test the coaches in practice, either.

"His sophomore year we were doing an 'over' drill the first day of practice, and Tom Young was the passer telling him to make a deep cut and lead him out so we can go backdoor," said former Assistant Coach John McFadden. "Everyone is doing it—denying, denying, denying. Phil doesn't feel like working too hard, so he comes out a little bit, and Tom completes the pass.

"He said, 'Phil, you have to close out. I want your hand up in the passing lane. I don't want them to be able to throw the ball.' They do it two more times, and both times Phil lets the guys catch the ball. Now we're at a test. Phil is saying to himself, 'This is just practice. I don't do this garbage.'

"The fourth time, Tom took the ball, and he throws a fastball that hits Phil on the side of the head, and he says, 'Get the fuck out of the gym. This is not your program. It's my program.' The players are standing there, stunned. I'm a little stunned too. He walks right up to Phil and says, 'Get the fuck out of here and don't come back.'

"Twenty minutes later, Abe Siviss (the head trainer) comes up and says, 'Sellers is down there in tears, and he wants to know if he can come back.'

"Whatever happened with Phil in practice, you knew that when push came to shove, when we had a really big game, that you could count on him always showing up. He was a warrior."

Sellers's ability to adapt to Young's coaching style—despite some rough stretches at times—was part of his maturing process, though he never lost his brash approach.

"Tom Young turned us boys into young men, and I give him a lot of credit," Sellers told Rutgers for its website when Young passed away in 2022. "He took all the guys that Dick Vitale recruited and took us all to the next step. He had no idea what he was getting into, but it didn't take him very long to lead us to success. Tom trusted me to lead the team. Tom and I used to joke all the time. He used to joke and remind me that he was the coach and I was the player. We used to laugh about things like that."

Practices were always intense, partly because Phil insisted on it, and partly because we had a team of winners who never, ever let up.

Everything was a war: thirty-second drills (where everyone lines up on the baseline and sprints to the other baseline and back three times), suicide drills, rebounding drills, and five-on-five games that we played as if the winner won a championship.

Given Phil's personality, one can imagine how challenging that could be for someone competing with him, especially if you were assigned to guard him in practice every day, as I was.

One time in particular stands out for me. We were playing a five-on-five scrimmage that pitted the starters (always in red) against the second team (in white). The ball went up, and Bruce Scherer and Phil fought for the rebound. Out of nowhere, Phil threw a massive elbow that landed on the side of Bruce's head. Down he went.

Everyone more or less stopped—except Phil, who grabbed the ball, stepped over Bruce, and started to dribble up court. I couldn't let that stand, so I raced over to Phil and grabbed him. He clearly wasn't pleased.

A mini-scrum started, and Coach Young immediately stepped in to stop it.

"Sellers, we don't need any of that crap on our court," he announced. "You can leave."

Everyone was stunned. Phil had just gotten thrown out of practice. Phil took it well because he understood by then that Young was clearly the boss. He left practice, and by the next day all was forgiven. But there was no denying Sellers' relentless intensity on the basketball court.

"Every time I would come into the game for Phil—he never wanted to come out of the game—I would ask him, 'Who do you have?' " said Steve Hefele. "He would mumble something I couldn't understand, because he was not happy about coming out. The guy I knew I had was the guy who scored the next basket, because nobody was guarding him."

For the younger players in particular, Sellers was someone to both admire and fear.

"That one-on-one, every day in your face—that was Phil's approach," said James Bailey. "I'd never experienced anything like that.

"To be honest, I was like everyone else—I learned to adapt and accept it and use it as a catalyst to improve. I knew every day at practice I could not come in and take a minute off. I would get more flak from Phil than I would from the coaches."

Sellers was actually one of the driving forces to get Bailey into the starting lineup, recognizing that the six-foot-nine freshman's rebounding and shot-blocking ability were the missing pieces for our team. Bailey gave us a dominant presence in the middle and could erase a mistake on the defensive end. He became the starter in our sixth game.

"I had no pressure from anyone about that situation except one individual—Phil Sellers," said Bailey. "Every day on the practice floor Phil would push the issue of me starting. He would say, 'What are you going to do? Are you going to take the spot? We need you to start.' You know how strong-minded Phil was. I got more pressure from him than anyone or anything else."

Stan Nance witnessed Sellers exerting pressure on Bailey to push himself to start on several occasions.

"Phil was always saying to Bailey, 'Hey, JB, when are you going to take that (starting center) spot?' " Nance said. "He would say it constantly to him. We would be in the car leaving the Barn, and he would turn to James and say to him, 'When are you taking that spot?' He knew James was the missing piece."

Sellers had a habit of letting officials know when a call did not go his way, which resulted in more than a few technical fouls but only seemed to further fuel him.

I still remember how he went off against USC his sophomore year in the Oklahoma City Tournament, scoring forty-three points against a team that was ranked No. 3 or 4 at the time. We lost that game, 82–81, but Phil practically willed us to a big upset.

In the Holiday Festival at Madison Square Garden during the 1974–75 season, Phil scored seventy-six points and drew nine charges in the three games. A game later, against LIU, he drew three charges. That willingness to take contact was part of what made him such a special player.

I am certain that if statistics were kept for charges taken, Phil Sellers would hold that record at Rutgers as well.

The 1976 ECAC Tournament final, in a packed Madison Square Garden with an NCAA tournament berth on the line, provided one of Phil's most memorable stretches. He took over the game late, challenging Beaver Smith three straight times down the stretch, and scored all three times as we beat St. John's.

"Phil was a nasty son of a gun on the court," said Nance. "He would elbow you and treat you like he treated opposing players during games. Off the court he was the greatest guy in the world and kind of soft-spoken. But he was a maniac on the court. I'm talking about punishing players. He would get into players' heads all of the time.

"Phil would kill me in practice with elbows and try to intimidate me, and Coach Young never called any fouls in practice. You had to learn to deal with it if you wanted to last."

Despite Rutgers's then–Assistant Coach Dick Vitale's relentless recruiting, Sellers originally committed to Notre Dame. But a change of heart eventually led him to Rutgers.

Phil passed away on September 19, 2023. In my mind, and in the view of the majority of Rutgers basketball fans, he remains the greatest player in school history.

SECTION 1:
STARTING 5

James Bailey #20

Hollis Copeland #34

Eddie Jordan #30

Phil Sellers #12

Mike Dabney #32

ROTATION PLAYERS

Steve Hefele #50

Mark Conlin #42

Bruce Scherer #24

Stan Nance #22

Mike Palko #52

Jeff Kleinbaum #44

Abdel Anderson #54

COACHING STAFF / MANAGERS

Managers: Scott Walton, Ken Eisler, Peter Horowitz

Tom Young Head Coach

Art Perry, Tom Young, Joe Boylan, John McFadden

Tom Young, Head Coach, Joe Boylan and
John McFadden Assistant Coaches

Tom Young and his White Towel

THE JOURNEY BEGINS

URING THE SUMMER PRIOR TO the 1975–76 season, most of the team followed a familiar routine. Most players headed back home, but some stayed in New Brunswick to work out at the Barn or at Livingston's gym.

I went back to Bayside, New York, to focus on two sports. I played four games a week in a summer baseball league on Long Island, and I worked out with my friend, Ira Kalter, at the P.S. 205 basketball courts across the street from the apartment buildings I grew up in. Ira knew I was working on developing my skills, so he passed me the ball a hundred times a day to try to get me better (what a friend).

Eddie Jordan and Phil Sellers stayed in New Brunswick for about three weeks working out at the Barn and enjoying summer life at Rutgers. Then, Phil left for Brooklyn and Eddie stayed at Rutgers and took summer courses. He also worked for his Uncle Ike at his Texico station in Plainfield, New Jersey. Near the end of the summer, Eddie went back to DC to see his family and play "serious" ball in his local playground, called Fort Stevens. Some NBA greats like Adrian Dantley and Kermit Washington often played there as well.

"I wanted to work on my ball handling because Coach Young made it clear to me that I was the point guard and I never did that in HS," Jordan said. "I am really glad I did it too."

Hollis Copeland was a two-sport athlete also, so his off-season time was divided as well.

"Right before school ended, I was doing the high jump and long jump with the (Rutgers) track team," Copeland said. "We could only do basketball camps and work out on our own. Five-Star Basketball Camp was one place I went to get better, and I worked out at Trenton State College (now College of New Jersey) as well."

Mike Dabney was able to hone his game closer to home as well.

"I played in two or three summer league games per week at Elmwood Park in East Orange (New Jersey). Dr. J (Julius Erving), Dave Cowens, and Tiny Archibald, and other NBA and ABA players came to the park for night games," he recalled.

Abdel Anderson, an incoming freshman, played in a nearby Belleville, New Jersey, park named Broad and Bay, "sometimes seven days a week," he said.

"On occasion Mike (Dip) Dabney would come with a friend of his and pick me up. That was great for me, because I got to play in high-quality games and also play with Dip on a regular basis. JB (James Bailey) would show up, and that was good for all of us too."

Bruce Scherer wanted to improve his strength and shooting, which were already strong, heading into his senior year.

"During the summer," he said, "I worked for my father in construction five days a week and then played basketball at Mountain Lakes High School three or four nights a week with players from Princeton and Seton Hall. The games were very competitive, and we all knew that we were going to play each other during the upcoming season, so we each wanted to be at our best."

Mike Palko had ended the previous year as a starter—he started the first five games of the 1975–76 season too—but that didn't deter him from wanting to take his game to the next level, focusing on his upper and lower body strength and also his shooting touch.

"I worked out every summer when I was in college," he said. "Going into my senior year, I took it up a notch, and I think it showed in the early practices."

Palko proved to be the ultimate team player, in my opinion, given how he reacted so graciously and unselfishly to being replaced by James Bailey after we won our first five games in the Final Four season.

He was, and is, always team first, and he came to New Brunswick in the best shape of his life his senior year.

Mark Conlin probably had the most difficult schedule of all of us. Immediately at the end of his freshman year, he revealed that he and his longtime girlfriend, Kathleen, were getting married.

I knew Kathleen pretty well because she visited Mark often and she was terrific. Little did I know, though, that Kathleen would become our team's social director and resident event planner, a role she continues to play to this day. Anything that has to do with our team, including birthdays, parties, or anniversaries, is sent to us from Kathleen with a note reminding us to attend. We never wanted to miss something that Kathleen promoted.

Stan Nance went home during the summer and was able to play with his brothers, who were terrific players in their own right. "We played ball every chance we got," said Stan. "I wanted to be as prepared as I could be because I expected everyone to be in great shape too."

The official first day of practice was always October 15. We were ready for it; there was no doubt about that.

The coaches knew we were best when we ran, so their goal was to get us into the best shape of our lives. Coach Young's practices were very disciplined, and every drill was timed on the scoreboard against the pool wall.

He might put us in a defensive "shell drill," for example, and set the game clock for twenty minutes. We stuck to that drill the entire time, no matter how well or how poorly we were doing it.

In between drills we would run all kinds of stomach-turning sprints. We would do thirty-second drills (which Young turned into twenty-seven-second drills when we got in better shape), suicides, sprints, and defensive stance drills. Because Young wanted us in top shape so we could press and run the break all the time, our intrasquad scrimmages featured five different full and three-quarter traps.

Coach Young was the perfect fit for our team. He recognized early on that our pronounced strength was our team quickness, so he designed our offense and defense around that.

As a high school coach for close to forty years myself, I have too often seen a coach insist on fitting his players into his system. Coach Young did just the opposite, and I believe it was one of his great strengths. Joe Boylan, his top assistant, was his ideal complement. He had a quiet strength that earned the respect of everyone he worked with. John McFadden was on Dick Lloyd's staff when Young took over, and Young made a great choice by keeping him on his staff. Coach McFadden is one of the brightest basketball minds I have ever been around, and his intensity at every practice and game influenced everyone on the team.

Art Perry, the other assistant coach, had played for Young at American University before coming to Rutgers with him. Perry was instantly loved by everyone in the program because of his honest, sincere, and straightforward approach. He also had a tremendous feel for the game.

The bottom line is this: By October 15, we were very eager to get going. We were focused and prepared. We worked six days a week, sometimes seven, two to two-and-a-half hours a day. Everything was designed to create a fast-paced attack and we concentrated on defense as well. The key to that preseason as far as I was concerned, was that we all bought in 100 percent.

When Young first got to Rutgers, he introduced an "organized fast break," something I had never seen before. He numbered each player, point guard was #1, off guard was #2, small forward was #3, the big forward was #4, and the center was #5. Anytime we went on a break, we needed to run it in a certain way. #1 would bring it up, #2 would go down the left side, #3 would go down the right side, #4 would follow #1 and go to the opposite foul line that #1 went to, and #5 would go right down the middle to the basket. Although breaks took on many forms in real life, each guy learned over time to fill his spot and did so with great speed and efficiency. It really worked well.

As the season approached, we began to look at our first few games. The first seven offered several challenges from the likes of Purdue, Boston College, Seton Hall, and Penn. Penn was coached by future

NBA Hall of Famer Chuck Daly. UConn and Temple looked to be formidable opponents as well.

A word about our "second team." All of us pulled for each other during every practice and game, no matter where we stood on the team, who played ahead of us, or who played behind us. The job of the guys who didn't start or didn't play much in games was to make it very difficult for the first team to beat us in practice situations and scrimmages. The harder we made it, the more it would help the starters in games.

We took that responsibility very seriously, and the scrimmages, like the games, often turned into basketball wars. On the occasions when we won a scrimmage or played great defense against the first team, we would quietly say among ourselves, "We are playing against one of the best teams in college basketball every day, and we are holding our own very nicely. We must be pretty good too."

The opening game of the season was at home, and we barely broke a sweat in a 100–60 rout of Bentley College. It marked the first of eleven times that we scored one hundred or more points that season.

I got the nickname "Mr. 100" because I scored the hundredth point seven of those eleven times.

A side note about that: I was getting way too much publicity for scoring the hundredth point as often as I did, but the crowd used to really get into it when we reached ninety-eight or ninety-nine points.

After I earned my nickname after a couple of early games, Bruce Scherer and Mark Conlin decided that if the situation arose again in one of our upcoming games, they were going to freeze me out. (It was all done in jest, I might add.)

So when we got to ninety-eight points against Pittsburgh on January 27, Scherer, Conlin, and I were in the game. Scherer got the ball at the foul line, and I made a cut that left me wide open going to the basket. I called for the ball, and Scherer looked right at me, smiled, and shot. For a moment I was annoyed, until I saw the guy who was guarding Bruce had managed to get a piece of the shot, causing it to fall short and drop into my hands.

I made the layup to get us to one hundred, the crowd cheered, and Scherer and Conlin stood there, shaking their heads in disbelief.

After dominating Bentley in our opener, we faced Purdue at Madison Square Garden, which we viewed as our home away from home.

The Boilermakers had a good squad (they would finish third in the Big Ten, with the league sending two teams to the Final Four that year) that featured an outstanding freshman guard named Kyle Macey, who had been named Indiana's Mr. Basketball in his senior year in high school. He transferred after that year to Kentucky, where he started at guard for the national champion Wildcats two years later. He was also the first Kentucky player to be a consensus SEC Player of the Year.

That game was a close contest until we pulled ahead at the end and won 81–73.

The game that followed, against Seton Hall at the Barn, was something truly special. It put our dynamic and potent offense on full display.

Seton Hall, coached by Bill Raftery, had some of the best players in the school's history on that roster. The team featured guard Nick Galis, who would go on to become a legend in the Greek basketball league and was inducted into the FIBA Hall of Fame; guard Greg Tynes, who went on to score 2,059 points in college; and another solid guard in Tom Flaherty.

Glenn Mosley, who would go on to become the nation's leading rebounder the next year and an eventual first-round NBA draft pick, was on that Pirates' roster as well. But he was suspended for that game due to an NCAA recruiting violation.

If you're a true Rutgers basketball fan, you know what happened that day. The game was just about over at halftime. Phil Sellers sat the final nine minutes (after scoring thirty-six points), as did the other starters, and we rolled to a 119–93 victory. That point total remains the highest in school history.

"We tried to play at a fast pace that day, which in retrospect was probably a mistake against that Rutgers team," said Raftery. "We had good team speed. We were always short up front both in height and depth. So that turned out to be a bad matchup for us."

Coach Young, who often kept his feelings about his team private, came out with a very prophetic statement to the reporters gathered in the postgame press conference.

"I was surprised to see them come out and run with us," he said. "I think it was the pressure of our defense that forced that. I really don't know just how good we are, but I know that we'll beat any team that tries to run against us."

What followed was a series of easy wins that started to hint that something special was going on.

We won 105–82 at Boston College, a team many predicted to be a power in the East that year. Then we handled the University of Pennsylvania, coached by Chuck Daly, at Madison Square Garden, beating them, 95–80, with our speed, pressure, and poise. After the game, Daly was duly impressed.

"It's early in the season, but from what I see, this Rutgers team could go undefeated," he said.

Coach Young wanted no part of that kind of talk that early in the season. When he heard about the quote, he spotted Daly in the hallway near the locker rooms and yelled to him, "Hey, Chuck! What are you trying to do to me?"

The national pollsters were slow to recognize our team in their weekly rankings. Often, a team that has never appeared in the rankings has to do something special to get in. Following the Penn game, the poll voters for the Associated Press Top 20 (there was not a Top 25 then) finally saw what we were doing.

In the December 15 AP Top 20, we appeared for the first time at No. 15. I remember some friends on campus saying we were ranked too low, but I was very happy to see our name among the top twenty teams in the country, and I knew that we could move up from there as long as we kept winning.

That was exactly what we did in the second half of December. We beat Connecticut at home, 96–83 (we would later meet the Huskies in the NCAA tournament), and then we cruised to a 95–62 win at Temple.

We knew the Connecticut game would test us, and the Huskies came out playing physically, with their best player, Tony Hanson, helping them to a 47–45 halftime lead. But during the second half, our speed, poise, discipline, and teamwork took over. Eddie Jordan was spectacular; he put the team on his back and scored twenty of his twenty-one points after halftime. He also got everyone else involved by dishing out eleven assists. Phil Sellers had twenty points, and our two freshmen, Bailey and Anderson, combined for thirty points (Bailey 16, Anderson 14).

We closed out December in the Poinsettia Classic in South Carolina, where we joined Furman, Georgia Tech, and The Citadel. Rutgers had never won a Christmas or Holiday Classic, so we all looked forward to those games. We gave it a good shot during the 1974 All-College Basketball Tournament in Oklahoma City, losing to fourth-ranked USC in a game that saw Sellers score a career-high forty-three points.

Playing as a ranked team now, we had no trouble beating The Citadel, 96–73, though we had our first injury scare during the game.

It takes a lot of variables to complete a special season, including great relationships between players and coaches, a sense of loyalty to one another, and unselfish attitudes. It also requires a little luck, especially when it comes to injuries.

So far, we had managed to dodge any serious injuries that could upset our rotation and team chemistry, but the percentages caught up with us when we played The Citadel. About eight minutes into the game, Mark Conlin, always a tenacious player, dove for a loose ball. His face slammed into an opposing player's knee, and he broke his nose.

Barely ten minutes later, Abdel Anderson was fighting for a rebound, and an opponent's forearm broke his nose too. Anderson, like Conlin, left the game and couldn't return.

Mark and Abdel pleaded relentlessly with the coaches, trainer, and team doctor to let them return to the game, but Coach Young wouldn't give in.

The setbacks were temporary, though. Team doctor Hyman Copelman, who was associated with Rutgers athletics for over fifty years and was at every game that year, averted a crisis by creating plastic masks for both players. The following night, Conlin and Anderson were available for the championship game against Georgia Tech.

The Yellow Jackets, a competitive ACC team, liked to shoot the ball quickly. We had watched them play the night before our game with the Citadel, so we felt we were in a good place.

Coach Young went over the matchups before the game, and we took the court with a great sense of purpose. One thing that really made us special that year was the focus we exhibited each and every night we played. Nobody took anything for granted, and everybody supported the big picture, which was to play to the best of our abilities and win.

Sellers and Dabney were our leaders; they were highly respected, and their focus and intensity permeated throughout the team. The game with Georgia Tech was competitive, but we controlled most of the play. The result was a closer-than-we-wanted 94–87 win.

As the calendar flipped to 1976, we headed to Florida to play Stetson. Coach Young had us arrive a few days ahead so we could take advantage of the sun and warmth there. (More on that game later.) He also had us stay in a hotel near the Disney complex, forty miles away.

We prepared for Stetson with a sense of satisfaction and pride. We were nine games into our season, and we had won them all. We had the school's first-ever in-season holiday championship on our resume. There was still a long way to go, but we all knew we were heading in the right direction. What was yet to come, though, was the building pressure that no other Rutgers team had faced before—or has since.

THE PRESSURE MOUNTS

W E HAD A PERFECT RECORD as the new year began, and everyone on the team had a sense that things were changing. The pressure to stay unbeaten was starting to build, and we were getting more national recognition. The media throng covering our games seemed to be getting larger, and the entire Rutgers campus was suddenly invested in our season.

Students were now camping out overnight before our home games—remember, we only played ten games at the Barn that year—to get tickets.

The coaching staff was obviously tuned in to all of this. They knew we needed some distractions every now and then to get our minds off basketball.

Months earlier, when Coach Young saw we'd be opening the new year against Stetson, he decided that we would stay near Disney World in Orlando, a little more than forty-one miles from the school's campus in Deland, Florida.

He had done a similar thing two years earlier when we opened the season against the University of Hawaii in Honolulu. We flew in six days before the game, giving us a chance to enjoy the weather and the sights. He held practice from seven a.m. to ten a.m. and then we had the rest of the day to ourselves. During the Stetson trip, we would likewise practice early and then head to Disney World to cut loose.

If there ever was a place that matched our personalities, it was Disney World. Not only were we miles away mentally from any basketball stress, but the visit to the "Happiest Place on Earth" also managed to coax a few of our more low-key personalities out of their shell. Steve Hefele, one of the quietest players on the team, decided it would be fun to test some of the rides Disney had to offer. Hefele, who was six-foot-five, convinced six-foot-two Mark Conlin, six-foot-eight Mike Palko, six-foot-three Eddie Jordan, and me (six-foot-two) to try the famous Mad Tea Party ride, which was designed for children. The five of us somehow squeezed into one teacup as passersby watched us make fools of ourselves.

Not only were five basketball players shoehorned into a teacup that wasn't designed for college basketball players, but the spinning motion had its desired effect on all of us, leaving the five of us dizzy as we exited the ride. We stumbled around for about five minutes like drunken sailors, trying not to get sick. (We were unsuccessful.)

"I thought it would be very cool to see five oversized guys squeeze into these bright colored teacups," said Hefele.

Palko, the tallest of us, had trouble staying in the teacup; his left leg dangled over the side. Jordan, meanwhile, spent the entire ride acting as if he was in deep pain.

The game against Stetson was a lot less painful and eventful, because it was never in doubt. We led from start to finish and won by twenty-one points. Sellers led the way with nineteen points, putting him within one point of two thousand for his career. What it signaled to me was how cohesive our team was getting.

When we returned to New Jersey, we faced a stretch of games against our traditional opponents, Fordham, Columbia, Bucknell, Lehigh, and Lafayette. Though we played these schools every year, critics saw this portion of the schedule as a reason to question our ranking and our validity as a team to be taken seriously on the national level.

Just a few years earlier, we were basically at the same level as those schools. Remember, we didn't start giving basketball scholarships until 1972.

We ignored the critical noise and won those games the way a top-tier team should. We routed Fordham, 93–55, then beat Columbia by twenty-nine, and then topped one hundred points against Bucknell, Lehigh, and Lafayette, winning those games by an average margin of twenty-seven points.

To that point, we had yet to experience a letdown—though our coaches never would have tolerated one if they sensed it happening.

Against Columbia, a game in which Dabney led the way with twenty-six points, our coaches were as intense as a staff can be in a game that we would win by twenty-nine. Not only was Coach Young hit with a rare (for him) technical foul for his remarks to an official, but Assistant Coach John McFadden got one as well.

The buzz prior to facing Bucknell at the Barn was palpable. We were 12–0, but more importantly, Phil Sellers was within reach of Bob Lloyd's Rutgers career scoring record. Lloyd, the brother of our first coach, Dick Lloyd, was Rutgers's first All-American basketball player. He had the school record for career points with 2,045, and Sellers needed eighteen points to become the new record holder (a distinction he still holds fifty years later).

The crowd was aware of Sellers's pursuit, raising the decibel level whenever he took a shot. The game was competitive until we put on one of our patented game-breaking spurts to end the suspense. With 11:55 left in the game, Sellers converted a layup that put him at the top of Rutgers's all-time scoring list.

The game was stopped, and with the crowd in a frenzy, Rutgers University President Dr. Edward Bloustein strolled to halfcourt. Holding the ball Sellers used for his historic basket, he spoke over the public address system.

"On behalf of Rutgers University and its friends, I congratulate you," Bloustein said.

After the game was over, Sellers remained at midcourt for almost an hour, signing autographs and telling stories to people who wanted to be around his "aura." As Phil's teammate, classmate, and friend, I feel privileged to have witnessed that historic moment.

Now at lucky 13–0, we faced a short bus ride to take on Lehigh in Bethlehem, Pennsylvania. Those bus rides—remember, we only had ten home games—often gave us a chance to partake in some locker room-type fun.

"The bus was like an extension of the locker room," said Scherer, who was never bashful about telling an off-color joke. "It was a safe place for all of us, a place where there was no press and the coaches generally ignored what we were talking about. Nothing was sacred, and cheap shots were the expected topics of every ride."

Jordan, one of our leaders even though he wasn't a captain yet, saw the bus rides as our personal and protected team space, a place where anything goes.

"Sometimes, if we were going somewhere and there was no practice or game scheduled when we got to our destination, a six-pack of some alcoholic beverage made it onto the bus," said Jordan. "My first taste of Southern Comfort, which became one of my go-to drinks, came on one of our bus trips."

The introduction of an adult beverage or two was Coach Young's way of rewarding us, while also allowing us to blow off some steam. (In 1976, the drinking age in New Jersey was eighteen, having been changed from twenty-one in 1973). The first time I experienced it was in my sophomore year, after a game at Madison Square Garden. On the bus ride back to New Brunswick, with everyone in a good mood following a victory, Louie, our bus driver, pulled over in front of a liquor store just before the Lincoln Tunnel, and Assistant Coach Joe Boylan hopped out. A few minutes later, Boylan came back onto the bus loaded with six packs of Michelob beer. Coach Young sent enough around for each player to have two.

"These are for you guys. Two beers never hurt anybody," Young announced.

Abe Siviss, our trainer, and Louie, who as far as I knew never had a last name, were on every bus trip. They would yell at each other about Louie's driving and Abe's pregame taping of players. Siviss had a distinctive, raspy voice that made us all laugh hysterically. Mike Palko did a spot-on impression of Siviss's voice, complete with hand gestures and phrases the trainer was known for. (Fifty years later Palko could still do that Abe Siviss impression. It made us laugh every time.)

Mike Palko and I graduated at the end of the Final Four year, but Abdel Anderson picked up where Palko left off to perfect his Siviss imitation.

The game at Lehigh was a good one for many reasons. We led from start to finish, playing with motivation, and James Bailey, the freshman center we knew we needed as the season progressed, really showed his potential and shot-blocking ability. Bailey had twenty-three points, ten rebounds and three blocks, while his classmate, Abdel Anderson, had ten points.

We headed home that night feeling good about ourselves—we were now 14–0—and the bus ride back became a scene out of a movie (remember *Animal House*).

Four nights later we returned to Pennsylvania to face Lafayette College in Easton; our focus for that game was on Todd Tripucka, a 6–2 guard from Bloomfield, New Jersey, who averaged 26.1 points per game that season.

If the name Tripucka sounds familiar, there's a reason: Todd's brother, Kelly Tripucka, was a star at Notre Dame and in the NBA, and their father, Frank Tripucka, was a quarterback at Notre Dame.

Entering the Lafayette game, we were ranked No. 7 in the Associated Press Top 20 poll (we would move up to No. 5 in the next rankings). We now had a bullseye on us wherever we went, but we brushed off the pressure, scored more than a hundred points for the fourth straight game, and rolled to a 113–79 win. Our point total set a record for a visiting team at Lafayette's Kirby Field House.

Dabney, who was playing really well and was leading the team with twenty-two points, came out of the game with eleven minutes to play as the margin widened over an overmatched Lafayette team.

Sellers chipped in with seventeen points, and every other starter had double figures—except James Bailey, who was busy blocking four shots, two of which he sent into the stands. Once again, our freshmen, Bailey and Anderson, had strong showings offensively as they combined for twenty-seven points.

We were reminded several times to keep up our intensity and not have a letdown for our next game against Pittsburgh in the Barn. The

Panthers were not postseason caliber, but they were a decent team—and those can be the most dangerous opponents at times because they have nothing to lose. Coach Young kept reminding us how capable they were.

We came out very strong, and I credit the crowd for a lot of that. We had been on the road for two games, and our fans were eager to let us know they were there for us,

Pittsburgh Coach Tim Grgurich apparently had not watched a lot of tape on us, because he made the same mistake other coaches had made earlier in the season.

"We haven't slowed the ball down all year," Grgurich said before the game, "and we've played against teams like Alabama, Notre Dame, and Marquette. I don't think we'll do it against Rutgers."

Big mistake. We ran Pittsburgh out of our gym in a 102–71 romp, improving our record to 16–0.

After the game, Grgurich told the media how impressed he was with what he had just witnessed.

"We have played Marquette and Notre Dame, and Rutgers is equal to them," he said. "It would be a hell of a game if they ever met. In every other game we have been able to keep it at our own pace. Tonight, Rutgers just ran over us."

It was pretty obvious that we were meant to run, and that philosophy started with our head coach.

"You know," Young said after the game, "if I asked these guys to play a game in the fifties, that would be criminal."

Dabney, always insightful after games, had perhaps the best take on what had just happened.

"I just don't see how a car that runs at fifty-five miles an hour can beat one that runs at ninety-nine miles per hour," he said.

Sellers came out playing great offense and great defense, blocking shots and taking charges as well as scoring. He not only scored seventeen points, but he had seventeen rebounds. He also spread the ball around, getting eleven assists for a triple-double.

Hollis Copeland credited Coach Young for instilling a defensive mindset into our star offensive player, knowing it would seep into the mindset of everyone else on the roster.

"Coach Young did a lot of talking to us about defense," he said. "All I wanted to do when I got here was score a lot of points. But he told me to learn from the others, and to look at what Phil was doing on defense, and to not sulk and worry about points. Now it's not even work. It's second nature. Fun and games."

It didn't take us long after the Pittsburgh game to turn our attention to rival Princeton, a school Rutgers had been playing against since 1869, when it beat the Tigers in America's first intercollegiate football game, which was played on the site that became the Barn.

The basketball teams had developed a heated rival as well. Watching Bill Bradley, the future New York Knicks great and US senator from New Jersey, battle with All-American Bob Lloyd and his backcourt partner, Jim Valvano, raised the stakes in the rivalry.

But these were different times. The rivalry took on a new slant because our team had become a national power, and Princeton had just made its first appearance in the Top 20 on the day of our game.

A word about Princeton's coach, Pete Carril. He was an outstanding coach ever since he started his career at Lehigh in 1966–67, and then moved to Princeton. Over his twenty-nine-year career at the Ivy League school, he posted a 514–261 record, a winning percentage of 0.663. What was truly impressive about what he accomplished was that he had that great success without scholarship players. He won the Ivy League title thirteen times and was invited to the NCAA tournament eleven times. In 1975 the Tigers won the NIT.

During the week leading up to the game, which would be played at Princeton's Jadwin Gym, our practices took on a new purpose. For the first time during the season, the "second team," as we were called, needed to play the same patient style that Princeton employed. That style, as everyone knew, was deliberate, with a lot of cuts and screens and, of course, backdoor passes. The fact that our philosophy was to deny all passes and use our quickness to disrupt those passes around the perimeter made us susceptible to the backdoor.

"For me, Princeton was difficult," said James Bailey. "It was more of a mind game. Princeton wasn't just about going out and playing. Princeton always seemed to have an attitude of 'let's go out there and see who is the smartest.' Everything they did was deliberate and precise and disciplined.

"We knew we were going to try to score the way we usually do. They were going to hold the ball and try to drag us into a low-scoring game. To me, that was one of the most difficult teams and style of play to get used to. Honestly, I disliked playing them. We were that fast-break, go, go, go team, and all of sudden they put brakes on that. It wasn't a fun game."

Assistants Boylan and McFadden, who were in charge of planning for an opponent's offense, emphasized that the second team should execute those backdoor cuts perfectly, and that we should take anywhere from forty-five seconds to a minute before looking to shoot to simulate Princeton's style.

"We were a unit that got very little credit, because our first unit was so good," said Stan Nance. "Oftentimes we would play the first team extremely tough, but Coach Young would simply blow the whistle and yell at the first team for playing like garbage."

That usually didn't faze the second team because it meant we were doing our jobs by making it difficult on the starters, simulating game conditions for them.

"Not getting credit is part of what we signed up for," said Nance. "We knew that making them work harder would make all of us better, and that was what we were all in to do."

The hype surrounding the Princeton game took on added significance when the Associated Press Top 20 poll came out the day of the game.

Though we had been making steady progress in the poll, we inexplicably dropped from No. 5 to No. 7 that day. Princeton, awaiting our visit, checked in at No. 19.

The media hyped the game into the battle for bragging rights in New Jersey and a clash between two ranked teams with opposite styles. We wanted to run at every opportunity, while Princeton was very deliberate, willing to hold the ball for what seemed like an eternity to get a good shot or a backdoor layup, making for the classic tortoise vs. hare showdown.

Bruce Scherer, who was from Parsippany, New Jersey, had a personal stake in playing Princeton too, because of a rivalry with the Tigers's Andy Rimol, a terrific player who had graduated from Princeton two years earlier. Scherer's Parsippany Hills High School team played against Rimol's Mountain Lakes High School teams for three years, and the two developed a great friendship as they not only played against one another but also worked out together in the summers.

So Scherer understood the significance of the Rutgers-Princeton rivalry.

"If you couldn't get up for the Princeton game, then you had no right to lace up your sneakers for any game," Scherer said. "They were an exceptionally well coached team, and they played a fundamentally sound game on offense and defense."

Jadwin Gym was an odd-looking arena that seemed more conducive to indoor track than basketball. It had a high ceiling, and the court was far from the stands on its deep side.

"When I first got there, I thought we were in an airplane hangar," said Nance.

Although it was not an intimate place, Princeton adapted to the environment quite well and usually gave opponents fits there.

On game day, the hype reached a crescendo, especially after a local radio station announced that this would be the first meeting ever between two New Jersey schools ranked in the AP Top 20.

To the surprise of only a few people, the game started out very slowly for us since we were thwarted from our up-tempo style.

Coach Young noticed it right away. "Both teams were tight in the early part of the first half, and we shot horribly," he said afterward.

Once the early nerves gave way and everyone settled in, both teams tried to exert their will. We took a 42–36 lead into the locker room at halftime.

The second half became the classic that many expected it to be. With 11:30 left to play, we were clinging to a two-point lead when Armond Hill picked up his fourth foul. That was significant, since Hill went on to be named Ivy League Player of the Year that season before embarking on an eight-year NBA career.

Coach Carril called a time-out after the foul call and directed his team to play keep away, to hold the ball unless there was an uncontested layup. Princeton went into its patented slowdown offense, and we were able to put our practices during the week to good use by resisting the urge to blindly overplay passes and risk giving up a backdoor layup.

Princeton held the ball for nearly four minutes as we clung to that two-point lead, until Mike Dabney, our lightning-quick guard, made a steal with a little more than five minutes to play that changed the entire tempo of the game.

Here's how Dabney described the situation:

"There was no shot clock, so they could just eat up the clock. I didn't make any moves toward intercepting any passes until I thought it was perfect timing. When they were stalling, I knew eventually the passer was going to relax and he was not going to pass the ball with speed or zip, because I never made an effort like I was going to try for a steal.

"I just timed it right. I think they kind of relaxed and I just stepped into the passing lane and was able to take it the other way for a layup. It kind of broke their backs."

We played the last five minutes with good energy and even better execution, a lot of it due to Mark Conlin's off-the-bench contributions. He stepped in for Ed Jordan, who had foul trouble, and played with poise and speed.

About the same time that Hill headed to the bench with foul trouble, Eddie Jordan did as well. Losing a key player at that juncture could have been costly, but one of the things that made our team special was our bench and our depth.

Coach Young didn't hesitate to put in Conlin when Jordan was whistled for his fourth foul, and Conlin picked up where Jordan left off. He was all over the court, making it very difficult for Princeton to maintain its rhythm.

"Mark played very well when I was out, and I loved it," said Jordan. "We needed something to pick us up at that time, and Mark gave it to us."

Rutgers won, 75–62, and there were good feelings all around as we improved to 17–0 and added a victory over a ranked opponent on the road to our burgeoning credentials.

"It was fun to be in a close game," said Dabney. "It showed where we were at, where we stand as far as pressure games are concerned."

Coach Young welcomed what was a rare test at that point, though Princeton did hold us to our lowest point total of the regular season.

"This was the kind of game we needed," Young said. "We have been winning by a lot, and to come to Princeton and beat them by thirteen is quite something. It was definitely good for us."

As we left Jadwin Gym and took the short ride back to New Brunswick, we knew we had just overcome a pretty significant hurdle. But we could not savor the win for very long.

We needed to get ready for West Virginia in three days, and the pressure of staying perfect was growing substantially. We were about two-thirds of the way through the regular season, but we knew we had several challenges ahead.

MAKING HISTORY

I T WAS BOUND TO HAPPEN. Unbeaten and unscathed through two-thirds of the regular season, we were due for a setback of some kind—an injury, a disciplinary problem, or some sort of letdown. No team I had ever played for, whether it was basketball or baseball, went through an entire season without facing an issue that affected everyone on the team.

When a team is "flat," it's an inexplicable feeling. It creeps up on you. It can happen to an individual or to an entire team. What sets the great players and teams apart from the merely good ones is how they fight through the malaise.

Our first "flat" game came against West Virginia at Madison Square Garden. It was the opening game of a doubleheader; Marquette played Manhattan in the second game. It's possible that the daunting presence of Marquette had something to do with our lost focus. Marquette was 14–1 at the time and had established itself as an elite team. Its roster was loaded with the likes of Butch Lee, Bo Ellis, Jerome Whitehead, and second-team All-American Earl Tatum, who was a senior. Lee, Ellis, and Whitehead formed the nucleus of a team that would deliver a national championship to Marquette a year later.

The Marquette team that was with us in the Garden this day would go on to finish 27–2 and lose to eventual national champion Indiana in the Mideast Regional championship game.

Whatever the reason, we did not come out against West Virginia with the same intensity and sense of purpose that forced the nation to take notice of us after our 17–0 start.

Coach Young was clearly troubled by our performance.

"I'm really, really concerned," he said after the game. "We made too many mistakes. We were up fifteen points in the first seven minutes of the game. We had a chance to blow them out early, and we didn't take advantage."

Though we lacked our usual energy, we built a 24–9 lead in the first seven minutes. But we let some of it slip away, and we headed into the locker room with a 45–36 lead at halftime. We started off well in the second half and increased our lead to thirteen points, but foul trouble became an issue and seemed to disrupt our rhythm. With 12:33 remaining, West Virginia tied the game, 57–57.

That's when our talented freshman, James Bailey, flashed some of the ability that would make him the No. 6 overall pick in the NBA draft three years later. He started his crucial sequence with a tap-in off a miss. He did it again thirty-five seconds later. Following yet another West Virginia miss, he grabbed control of the rebound and fired a quick pass up court to Mike Dabney, who swished a corner jumper.

But West Virginia would not go away and drew within 61–60. That was when our alarm clock finally went off—a jumper by Steve Hefele, a layup and free thrown by Bailey, an eighteen-foot jumper by Eddie Jordan, a twenty-foot jumper by Hollis Copeland. In typical fashion, with the type of dazzling offensive burst we had become known for, we were suddenly up ten, and West Virginia was a beaten team. The final score was 86–76.

"I think we were trying to go too fast," Mark Conlin said afterward. "We'd get the ball downcourt, and after one pass we were going to the basket. We should have been passing more."

Mike Dabney said Rutgers was "too anxious."

"I thought they would be easy," said Jordan. "Some teams you are ready for. I mean really ready. But against some, you just go out and see what happens."

The good news about our "uneven" performance was the distribution of the scoring. Jordan and Copeland each had eighteen points, followed by Bailey's fourteen, Dabney's thirteen. and Sellers's eleven.

Navy was next, in the Barn, and this was ten years before the great David Robinson would elevate the Middies' program to heights it had not experienced before and hasn't since. This was not a good Navy team.

Even so, Dabney and Jordan served up a reminder of why they were one of the best backcourt duos in the country. Dabney was spectacular—running, shooting, passing, and playing stellar defense. His game totals were among the best of his career. He scored twenty-seven points, seven rebounds, eight assists, and a crowd-pleasing block that landed in the first row of the student section. Jordan complemented his performance with eighteen points, seven assists and five steals in an 86–71 victory.

It was almost impossible to block out the crowd's chants of "undefeated" that day, drawing even more attention to what we were trying to accomplish.

I remember vividly that the practices before our next game—at home against Delaware—were more challenging than usual (and that's saying something). I felt that Coach Young was trying to send us a message, and that turned out to be the case.

"We tend to practice harder before a game we should not be tested in," Young said the day before the game. "We get more accomplished with a sterner preparation against a team like Delaware. Our approach is definitely different in a situation like this."

The game followed our expectations. We rolled to a 110–87 win, and, yes, I scored the one hundredth point again.

But danger awaited when Manhattan came to the Barn five days later.

It seemed as if everywhere we went on campus, people talked about us going undefeated.

"Last week I walked into one of my classes, and the professor stopped what he was doing to congratulate me on our latest win," Stan Nance said. "He said that everyone, including all of the Rutgers staff members, were pulling for us to go undefeated. It was the same every-where I went."

If you asked me if I felt the pressure to go undefeated was getting to us, I would have to say no. We were a confident group, and we were riding one of those magical runs that showed no signs of stopping. But that was about to change when we took the floor against Manhattan.

Practices leading up to the game had their usual intensity, except for one thing: Eddie Jordan was nowhere to be found. He missed our first practice, and most of us figured he was ill.

Coach Young didn't make things easy on us. The workouts were extremely difficult, and it was clear he was not happy with what had transpired with Jordan. Most of us were in the dark about his absence.

We finally learned that he was recovering from a lingering knee injury suffered in the Delaware game. No one questions an injury—especially a rare one to a gamer and star like Jordan—but we couldn't understand why he didn't come to the gym for treatment or contact anyone.

The intrigue peaked the day before the game when Jordan showed up to practice and Coach Young announced he would sit out the game for disciplinary reasons.

Jordan said it was simply a lack of communication that created the situation.

"It's a very simple story," he said years later. "It was really just immaturity on my part. I didn't party too hard or anything like that. I didn't do anything wrong, as has been reported for years since that time. I had hurt my knee. The doctor told me that if I wanted to play the next game, I needed to stay off it for a couple of days.

"So what I did was stay in my dorm room. I wanted to be ready to play. So I stayed in my room the entire time with my leg up, as the doctor said. Back then, there was one phone for the whole dormitory. I was upstairs on the fourth floor, and the phone was on the first floor. Whoever called me to come to practice, I never got the message. I as-sumed the doctor told the coaches that I was staying off my feet, but that never happened either.

"On Thursday, I showed up to practice, and Coach Young was furious at me, saying, 'Nobody could find you.' He told me that I would sit out the Manhattan game, and that was it."

That wasn't it though. Just before the opening tip, the overflow crowd—the fire marshal was apparently in a very good mood that day—was in its usual raucous state. But the mood became a little subdued when the starting lineup was announced and Jordan wasn't in it. Mark Conlin was replacing him.

Adding to the confusion was that Jordan was in uniform and showed no signs of being affected or restricted by his knee during warm-ups.

Manhattan was clearly ready to play, hoping to prove that its 11–10 record was the result of a demanding schedule; six of their ten losses had come against ranked teams: Indiana (No. 1), Marquette (No. 2), Louisville (No. 10), Notre Dame (No. 13), and St. John's (No. 14) twice.

We went into the locker room leading 43–33 after a hard-fought first half. But what happened in the second half was a stark wake-up call, exacerbated by the absence of Jordan. With two minutes and fifteen seconds remaining in a highly competitive second half, we led 78–73, and we had the ball. All we needed get to 21–0 was to run out the clock.

Coach Young called a time-out and instructed us to go into a four-corners stall—the one Phil Ford and Coach Dean Smith made famous in North Carolina. But it was an uncharacteristic style of play for us. Mark Conlin got called for a five-second violation for holding the ball, largely the result of Manhattan turning up its defensive pressure. In the final minute, Manhattan's Steve Grant connected on a deep jumper. Then he intercepted a long inbounds pass and found teammate Tom Lockhart, who averaged 20.3 points and 10.0 rebounds that year). Lockhart sank his shot, narrowing the score to 78–77.

In the waning thirty seconds, Manhattan's Chris Dye came up with a tipped ball that also resulted in Conlin picking up his fifth foul, sending him to the bench.

Dye, who connected at 78.2 percent from the foul line that year, made the first of his two free throws, but he missed the second one. Sellers got the rebound, but his last-second shot rimmed out, sending the game into overtime.

During the time-out, with thirty seconds left after Conlin fouled out, there was quite a lively discussion in our huddle, easily the most intense one of the season. The crowd was chanting "Eddie! Eddie!" the paint chips were fluttering from the ceiling, and Assistant Coach Joe Boylan had to break it to Jordan that it was a matter of principle, that he had to sit out the entire game as his punishment.

That's when the team stepped in. We tried to convince Coach Young that Jordan had certainly learned his lesson, that he shouldn't be penalized further for his actions, and that losing the game would penalize all of us. Sellers and Dabney made impassioned pleas to the coaches, explaining that benching Jordan for nearly forty minutes was sufficient discipline for a misunderstanding. I really liked that reasoning. I knew that sitting for as long as he did was torture for Jordan.

The players' appeals seemed to win over the coaching staff. Young turned to Jordan and said, "Go in now." Jordan went to the scorer's table, and the ovation was deafening. It rocked the old Barn from the rafters. But his transition back to playing wasn't exactly smooth.

"When I first touched the ball, it felt like a square cinderblock," Jordan said after the game. "I took the first shot I had, and it missed everything. This was a very tight game, and it felt so weird. I don't know if anything I did helped the team in the end, except by me being there."

Jordan took control of the offense with his ballhandling and leadership skills, leading us to a 14–3 run and a 92–81 win in overtime.

"After Eddie settled down, he ran the show for us as he always does," said Young.

Sellers, who shared scoring honors with Dabney with twenty-six points apiece, also had fourteen rebounds and three steals. His postgame message was that he hoped the team learned from its great escape.

"A close game like this will give us a lot of incentive not to take anyone lightly the rest of the way," said Sellers. "Manhattan played a really good game. We made our mistakes, and they capitalized on them."

Coach Young looked drained after it was over and was heard telling Coach Boylan on the way out of the building, "I'm just happy to get the hell out of here with a win."

Given the events of the previous week, I think everyone felt the same way. We now had just five games left in our mission to become just the nineteenth team in modern NCAA history to go undefeated in the regular season.

We were also acutely aware that the calendar would turn to March in a little over two weeks. But the schedule ahead came first, and that meant dispatching Syracuse, American University, William & Mary, LIU, and St. Bonaventure. Two of those games would be at home, two at Madison Square Garden, and one on the road.

We knew we could win all of those games, but now we had to deal with more than just the opposition. We were carrying a "going undefeated" albatross around our necks every day now.

Up until now, going 26–0 seemed so far away; it was not something we usually paid attention to. But now it was getting closer to becoming a reality, and people would ask about it whenever we were in the company of friends or fans.

To add to the pressure, the media, specifically the newspapers that covered us, mentioned it prominently in every article. It was starting to seep into our consciousness as a result. Each game we played now could be the one where we stumbled. And as the media also noted, each team that remained on our schedule had nothing to lose.

"Teams come psyched to play us now," Young said. "They jump higher and shoot better."

Syracuse, our next opponent, was an example of what Coach Young meant. We were a clearly superior team, and we had them in the Barn, but the 93–80 final score was hardly a work of art in our minds.

During the days leading up to the game we worked on slowing down after we got a lead. But our execution left Coach Young clearly dissatisfied.

"We worked on taking the air out of the ball when we got a lead late in the game, but obviously our kids didn't learn a damn thing," he said after the game.

But we were 22–0 now.

American, the school Young left to coach Rutgers, was our next opponent—a Saturday afternoon game at Madison Square Garden— and it played a much more inspired game than its eventual 9–16 record would indicate.

"We don't have anything to lose," American Coach Jim Lynum said on the morning of the game. "If we hang in there and keep it close to the end…well, who knows?"

The game mirrored some others we had played recently, with more turnovers than usual and spotty defense. We played well in spurts, but we continued to have trouble slowing down the ball when we needed to. Although we won the game handily, 94–79, Young once again was less than impressed with our effort.

"We keep trying to score when we don't have to score," he said. "Our kids are used to running, and they find it difficult to stop. If we don't learn soon, it will cost us a ballgame."

We left the Garden knowing we would be back a week later to play LIU, and we were confident that we would be part of the four-team field for the ECAC Tournament there on March 4 and 6, with the winner earning an automatic bid to the thirty-two-team NCAA tournament. Stopping at the liquor store outside the Lincoln Tunnel had now become part of our routine after playing in the Garden, and Coach Boylan loaded up with Michelob beers for all of us.

Our next game, at William & Mary, worried many of us. We knew they had some good players and that they always played well at home.

Dabney, our co-captain, would have no part of our pregame angst. He was spectacular, scoring a career-high thirty-three points, with six rebounds and seven assists. Though William & Mary trailed us by just one point, 35–34, during the first half, we went on a 13–5 run for a 50–41 halftime lead.

In the second half, we steadily increased our lead, which was highlighted by Eddie Jordan scoring his thousandth career point. We survived our last road game with a 100–90 win.

Sellers scored a hard-earned twenty-two points as William & Mary double- and sometimes triple-teamed him.

"We have never played a better, quicker team," William & Mary's coach, George Balanis, said. "They are a great, great team, but I think they found out that we have a few players too."

Now 24–0, we returned to Madison Square Garden to face a solid LIU team coached by Paul Lizzo. LIU had lost three of its previous four games, but it had played well in several key games during the season. It won the All-College Tournament in Oklahoma City, beating Long Beach State, Eastern Kentucky, and Centenary, which was ranked in the Top 20 at the time. LIU had also soundly beaten Manhattan—the same Jaspers who took us to overtime—by a score of 88–71.

The game was unique in that both teams knew we would play each other again just four days later in the ECAC Tournament. The four-team field (an automatic NCAA tournament berth went to the winner) had already been announced.

"I consider it an honor to be able to play Rutgers twice," said Lizzo. "This gives us two chances to knock them off, and they are the No. 3-ranked team in the country, which they certainly deserve. If I had my druthers though, I'd prefer playing anyone but Rutgers. They're a hell of a team."

Young wasn't as enthused at the prospect of playing the same team twice in four days.

"I'm not looking forward to it," he said after practice the day before the game.

We started the game as we had started many others, building a seventeen-point halftime lead. But as had been the case too often during our recent stretch of games, that lead was whittled to 56–50 after LIU, led by high-scoring forwards Ernie Douse and Nate Revels, went on a 14–3 run.

During that run, Sellers was whistled for his fourth personal foul. Then Dabney picked up his fourth too, with 14:31 to play. That's when our depth took over and brought us home victorious. James Bailey scored seventeen points, Hollis Copeland was dominant, scoring fourteen points and pulling down eleven rebounds, Eddie Jordan had fourteen points, and Abdel Anderson came off the bench to score thirteen points. Even with foul trouble, Dabney had a team-high nineteen points in the 103–97 victory. It was the tenth time we hit the hundred-point mark.

Coach Young was particularly pleased with how we responded with Sellers and Dabney in foul trouble.

"We're obviously not a one- or two-man team," he said. "Jordan, Bailey, and Hollis probably played as well as anybody on our club."

The bus ride home was unusually quiet, perhaps owing to the reality that we had one more game of unfinished business. Once we returned to New Brunswick, the quiet quickly gave way to the buzz and excitement around campus that seemed overwhelming at times.

At 25–0, we would put our quest for a perfect regular season on the line two days later at home against St. Bonaventure. The game turned out to be as memorable—and nerve-racking—as any we played that regular season. The pressure on us to finish what we had started had now reached a crescendo, and we couldn't let ourselves or our fans down now.

THE ST. BONAVENTURE ESCAPE / LET THE BELL RING

WHY DOES IT SEEM LIKE the final obstacle to completing a historic quest is always the toughest one? On March 1, 1976, all that stood between us and the first perfect regular season in the New York metropolitan area since Columbia in 1950–51 was a home game against St. Bonaventure.

But there were warning signs everywhere, and to Tom Young they were practically screaming danger in large neon.

"We were too (psyched up)," Coach Young said months later after everything was done. "I tried to calm them down before the game, but I couldn't. This was the last one, the big one, and I couldn't get them down. They were really (psyched up)."

As if our bid for perfection wasn't dramatic enough, the game was punctuated by a controversial late foul call on St. Bonaventure guard Jim Baron. A half-century later, Baron insists it was a bogus call.

Let me set the scene: After trailing 75–68 with 6:08 to play, and with the specter of 25–1 instead of 26–0 looming over us, we staged a furious comeback and went on to outscore the Bonnies 17–5 the rest of the way. But we faced a serious challenge with that seven-point deficit that threatened to undermine our dream season.

"At that point we knew it was time for us to turn it on, or else," said Sellers, who finished with twenty-five points and thirteen rebounds.

A short jumper by Sellers gave us an 80–79 lead with 1:40 to play. Then Baron hit a free throw to force an 80–80 tie. One second later,

Abdel Anderson got fouled on the inbounds pass and calmly sank both ends of a one-and-one to put us back in front, 82–80.

Then things got very interesting.

Following a St. Bonaventure turnover with forty-eight seconds to play, Young took out James Bailey and inserted me. At first, I thought he was kidding. I hadn't played very much in three or four games, and now I was going in for the final forty-eight seconds of our biggest game of the season?

We were instructed to hold the ball and to force the Bonnies to come after us as the seconds slowly melted off the game clock. As the clock ticked down to thirty seconds, we were clinging to that two-point lead. Dabney was dribbling near the scorer's table just inside the halfcourt line when Baron reached around and slapped the ball away, redirecting it to guard Glenn Hagan, who threw it back to Baron, who went in for an uncontested layup that would have tied the game.

But referee Norm Van Arsdale blew his whistle to signal a foul as Baron was on his way to the basket. Baron was irate, slamming the ball on the court and confronting Van Arsdale about the call. Of course, the foul stood, and Dabney went to the foul line to shoot a one-and-one. He sank both free throws to make the score 84–80 and put the game away.

To this day, Baron believes it was a legitimate steal.

"The steal that I made on Dabney was as clean as a steal can be," said Baron, who went on to win 462 games as the head coach at four Division I programs. "I'm from New York, and we would make that play all the time. We would reach around the guy's back and knock it out. No one ever called that a foul.

"I reached around, knocked it back to my teammate, Glenn Hagan, and took off. He passed it back to me, and I took it toward the basket. When I got to the foul line, I heard something but finished the play. Then I saw that the ref had called us back because he called a foul on me. I was beside myself.

"What did I do, touch his fingernail? No, I got it clean. How can I hit his hand if his hand was on top of the ball and I swiped it from the side? My hand could not hit his hand that way."

Dabney saw it differently, of course.

"It was a slight foul, but he did get my hand," Dabney said. "I didn't have a problem with it at all, because it was a foul."

Coach Young was more philosophical about the key call.

"Was it a foul or wasn't it a foul?" he said. "To go undefeated, you're going to need a little luck, and you need to get a call now and then."

There was a lot of relief and exhaling—and, of course, some wild celebrations—after that 85–80 win. Over the years I have had more people than I can count come up to me and tell me they were at the game. If everyone who claimed to be there was actually there, the attendance would have had to be announced at ten thousand. Maybe more than that.

Now, back to the narrative.

The two-and-a-half days between the LIU game and the St. Bonaventure game were as hectic as any basketball lead-up I have been involved with. The entire coaching staff tried to get us to stay focused on the opponent, not on the stakes. But it wasn't easy. I was living in Century Apartments on Easton Avenue with Bruce Scherer, Brian Perkins (who at one time was recruited by Rutgers), and Bob Merker, who was on the tennis team. We were all close friends, and we tried to keep to our routine, especially with classes, as much as possible.

Walking to class on Monday, the day of the St. Bonaventure game, was like an out-of-body experience. It didn't seem real. People would stop me to wish us luck or to ask about St. Bonaventure and talk about how good they were.

Truth be told, they were a very good team that went on to finish 17–10 and would win the NIT the next year, beating Rutgers in the first round.

"I'm glad we are playing the last game at home," Young told the media that descended on our campus and tiny gym before the game. "Nobody deserves seeing the last game more than our students or fans. It's the proper place for us to be playing."

The day before the game, several players were asked to do radio spots with WRSU, the school's student station, or WCTC, the New Brunswick station that carried our games.

On the day of the game, it was very difficult to ignore the excitement, energy, and anticipation swirling around us. When I walked into my eight a.m. class that day, people stood up and clapped. You would have thought I had the answers to our next exam. All they wanted was to wish me luck.

After class, I met Scherer and Steve Hefele for breakfast at the Commons, and as we walked up College Avenue from Scott Hall, we noticed a line wrapped around the Barn—twice. We decided to cut in near Tinsley Hall and go the back way.

When Scherer and I arrived at the gym for the final home game of our Rutgers careers, it was more emotional than I expected. I had played there for four years and considered it the best home-court advantage you could ever want.

For the five seniors who had helped elevate the program to unprecedented heights—Sellers, Dabney, Scherer, Palko, and me—the Barn had been a special place for four years. I was a role player, but people gave me unwavering support, sometimes slapping my hand as I ran by them during the game. The fans were literally on top of you, so interaction with them wasn't uncommon.

"I was definitely emotional about this being our last home game," said Scherer. "When I looked out to the crowd from the side door we were about to run through, I thought back to the very first time I did this, four years ago against Georgetown. I had to collect myself seconds before we came out, for sure."

Palko was able to keep his emotions in check because he was laser-focused on one thing: winning the game.

"I was all business that night," he said. "I was singularly focused on beating St. Bonaventure and going undefeated. Nothing else concerned me."

As I went through the back door of the gym, as I had done countless times before, I was immediately struck by what was going on in the annex to my left. Our opponents usually used that back gym for warm-up shooting and dribbling before games, but not on this night. Instead, row upon row of tables had been set up the length of the court with phones and chairs every three feet apart. An overflow crowd of media was expected, and there was nowhere else to put them.

We went down to our cramped locker room, and I was taken aback when I walked in. Up against the far wall was a seven-by-seven-foot stage with a camera next to it. It was obviously there for postgame interviews and the expected locker room celebration.

When we walked up to the entrance to the gym, the crowd noise was ear-splitting—so loud, you could feel the steps shaking as we took the court. It was so loud, it was almost impossible to communicate with teammates or coaches when we ran out onto the floor. The whole Barn was shaking. The pep band could barely be heard over the noise.

We warmed up to a drill we called single exchange, which preceded our layup line. I was taking it all in as I also tried to focus on staying calm and in the moment. My parents were seated in their usual spot; their simple presence helped me suppress my nervousness.

After St. Bonaventure's starting lineup was announced, Rutgers paid tribute to the senior class by announcing me, Scherer, Palko, Dabney, and, finally, Sellers. The five of us took it all in and then came together with our hands in the middle.

In the days leading up to this game, we heard that the St. Bonaventure players were very happy that we'd survived overtime to beat Manhattan two weeks earlier. They wanted to be the ones to hand us our first loss, and they came in confident that they would do it.

They backed up that confidence in the first half; we had a slim 39–37 lead at the break.

"We showed no patience in the first half," Young said afterward. "You expect that to happen for the first seven or eight minutes in a game like this, until the players settle down, but we never settled down in the first half."

We started strong in the second half, hitting our first four shots from the field. But St. Bonaventure rallied to force a 54–54 tie. It was obvious to all of us now that we were going to have to work to earn this win.

It went back and forth for the next seven minutes until the Bonnies took a 75–68 lead with 6:08 to play. Sellers, Copeland, and Dabney answered with three consecutive jumpers to get us back to 75–74 with 4:30 remaining.

"We didn't lose our poise," said Young. "If we had lost our cool and started to take foolish chances in the last few minutes, we would have lost the game."

It was tied, 80–80, when Anderson calmly hit two free throws for an 82–80 lead before that costly St. Bonaventure turnover that would lead to the foul call on Baron.

Following a time-out, Coach Young tapped me on the shoulder and said, "Go in for Bailey, and make sure that we hold that ball." Hold that ball? I had to make sure I was going to hold my lunch!

When we took the ball out at halfcourt, we were in a straight line in front of the inbounder. On the slap of the ball, the first guy in the line goes either left or right, and each guy after him goes in the opposite direction of the guy in front of him. Since I was last in the line, I was sure that if I got the inbounds pass, I would be able to set up things and make sure everyone was in our delay game. Sure enough, on the break, each guy scattered in a different direction, and I went down the middle and got the ball.

As I brought the ball up, everyone in the crowd—even my parents—was probably holding their collective breath, hoping for the best but bracing for the worst with me suddenly running the point. After I brought the ball up court, I passed to Sellers, who then passed back to Dabney near midcourt. That's when Baron reached for the steal and set off the whistle that still causes debate.

"It was a close call," Young said. "I'm just glad they called it our way."

St. Bonaventure Coach Jim Satalin called it "the key play in the game."

Dabney, a dependable foul shooter his entire career, made both free throws for an 84–80 lead, and Hollis Copeland made a free throw in the waning seconds to make the final score 85–80.

St. Bonaventure missed two shots in its final possession before James Bailey used his left hand to block a shot back to midcourt as the buzzer sounded. As Bailey was soaring for the block, the stands emptied. Fans rushed the court, and the players scrambled through the delirious mob to get back to the locker room.

Students were climbing the baskets as they were being raised up for storage. Everyone, it seemed, was jumping around on the court to celebrate.

We headed directly for the locker room to escape any problems. I remember watching TV a few nights later as they showed the end of the game. As we scrambled off the court, the cameras caught Palko's face. His reaction was one of pure joy. He was smiling broadly and was waving his arms uncontrollably in celebration.

I had never seen that side of Palko, and I loved it.

The statistics for the game were what you would expect. Sellers led the team with twenty-five points and thirteen rebounds; Dabney had nineteen points and six assists; Jordan had sixteen points and nine assists; Copeland had eleven points, eleven rebounds, and two blocks. Bailey and Anderson combined for seventeen points and three rebounds.

They all met the moment when we needed them to. That was how we stormed back with a 17–5 run to win the game over the final 6:08.

Dabney sat on his stool for almost two hours after the game, seeming to be savoring every bit of the moment.

"The pressure is off now," he said. "The undefeated season is behind us, and it's going to be a lot of fun now."

What happened in the hours that followed the game was a scene that most people at Rutgers had never seen before—and have not seen since.

Immediately after we left the locker room, we were summoned to the men's basketball office on the second floor of the Barn. There, President Edward Bloustein, Athletic Director Fred Gruninger, the coaches, and players gathered.

We looked out the window and saw thousands of fans gathered below to celebrate. The New Brunswick Police Department estimated that there were close to ten thousand people reveling in the historic moment.

We were instructed to go to the window, one player at a time, so we could wave and shout and acknowledge the crowd as it roared back in approval.

Then we were hustled to a waiting bus that drove us down College Avenue to Old Queens, the oldest extant building on the New Brunswick campus. Once there, we had earned the unique privilege of ringing the bell that Colonel Henry Rutgers donated to the school in 1825, an honor the school reserved for special occasions.

The bell rang twenty-six times, once for each victory.

Back on the bus, the scene was unreal. People were reaching inside the open windows to touch us. The chant of "We're number one!" drowned out everything. I saw Jordan and Dabney reaching their hands out to people as the bus was moving, and the fans responded by climbing the side of the bus to make contact with us.

The bus was going slowly, and fans climbed up and clung to it as if they were hanging on to the side of a San Francisco trolley car. It was total mayhem—and pure joy.

(A personal note: I always thought we had the best pep band of any school we encountered, and our cheerleaders, led by captain Nancy Cramer, never failed to get the fans involved when we needed their support the most. They were out there with the rest of the crowd, cheering and leading chants.)

The players headed to Olde Queens Tavern that night for more than the bar's famous pizza, closing the place down during what would be a rare time to just kick back and share stories with teammates and fans. But it wouldn't take long for us to get back our focus. We had a rematch with LIU in the ECAC Tournament in three days at Madison Square Garden. Looming was St. John's, the team we would eventually meet in the championship game, with an automatic berth in the thirty-two-team NCAA tournament up for grabs.

PHIL VS. BEAVER

E VERYONE IN OUR PROGRAM KNEW what was at stake on March 4 in the opening game of the ECAC Tournament at Madison Square Garden. The winner of the four-team event would gain automatic entry (and a preferred seed) to the thirty-two-team NCAA tournament. LIU was our first opponent, but St. John's was looming.

We had beaten LIU during the season, so we were confident that the championship game would be between us and St. John's, which, as it turned out, also wound up in the NCAA tournament with an at-large bid.

So what was the big deal if both Rutgers and St. John's wound up in the NCAA tournament anyway?

Just this: Winning would get us a first-round game in Providence, Rhode Island, against Princeton, which we beat on the road during the regular season.

St. John's was shipped to South Bend, Indiana, to face unbeaten, No. 1-ranked Indiana, the eventual national champion.

That proved to be the difference between having a manageable path to the Final Four and being one-and-done.

Following the tense victory against St. Bonaventure to end the regular season, we took most of Tuesday off before we met for a short practice. Coach Young reminded us that we were going into a new season and that things could end abruptly with a subpar performance.

That was also when we learned that Coach Young had been named Sporting News Coach of the Year. It was a well-deserved honor. He was the perfect fit for Rutgers, and he led us with toughness and honesty. There was only one boss, he liked to remind us, and nobody ever questioned him. He was direct to a fault, and he looked you in the eye whenever you talked to him.

An example of his directness and honesty was how he dealt with me a year earlier. I had played quite a bit as a freshman and sophomore, but my playing time was steadily dwindling as a senior. Since Young had an open-door policy for all of us, I decided to ask him if there was anything I could do that I wasn't doing.

We sat down in his office, and I asked him if there was something I could do to get more minutes. Coach Young looked me in the eyes and asked me a few questions that turned out to be his answer.

"Jeff," he said, "it is clear that most of your time has been given to Steve Hefele, correct?"

I nodded in agreement.

"So what year are you and what year is Hefele?"

I said Hefele was a freshman and I was a junior.

"How tall are you, and how tall is Hefele?"

I didn't have to answer. He knew I was six-foot-two, and Hefele was six-foot-five.

"Who is the better shooter between the two of you?"

He knew the answer to that one too. I told him Hefele was clearly better.

Hefele was also the better rebounder and ballhandler, he said. I could not dispute either point.

Finally, Young asked, "Who is the better defensive player between the two of you?"

I almost jumped out of my seat. "Coach," I said, "I think I am every bit the defensive player as he is."

Young grinned and said he agreed.

"So given all that," he said, "who do you think should get the bulk of those minutes?"

The answer was obvious, but before I could answer, he continued.

"Hefele has taken some of your minutes, and now you have two choices. You can go around and sulk and become a distraction to the team, or you can work like hell to be ready when you are called on to play. And when that time comes that you are called, and if you are not ready, you will never be called on again."

I stood up, shook Coach Young's hand, and promised him that I would never be a distraction and that if I was asked to contribute, I would be ready.

That is what you want from your coach: honesty and fairness. I took that policy with me when I began my own high school coaching career.

We all loved and respected Coach Young. There isn't a guy from our team who doesn't miss him every day.

But back to the ECAC Tournament.

The LIU game was just what we needed to resume our dominant ways. We came out strong, playing confident and loose, and we were able to keep our focus in a 104–76 romp.

Coach Young substituted freely, as he usually did when he felt we were in control of a game. He put me in with five minutes to play, and I went on a rampage. Just kidding! I scored eleven points and connected once again for the hundredth point, the seventh and last time I would manage that during the season.

In the second game of the doubleheader, St. John's beat St. Peter's, 75–67, to set up the showdown we all anticipated.

The meeting between the two best teams in the metropolitan area would live up to its hype and expectations, largely because of the epic one-on-one battle that Sellers and St. John's senior Beaver Smith staged over the final six-plus minutes.

Both are gone now—Sellers passed away in 2023, and Smith in 2018—but the show they put on with the game on the line remains one of the great stretches of college basketball in Madison Square Garden history.

Sellers, the All-American from Brooklyn, and Smith, from Rockville Centre on Long Island, had known each other since before college, so the foundation for a personal rivalry was there already.

The funny thing is, their late-game, one-on-one confrontation almost never materialized. St. John's Coach Lou Carnesecca initially gave 6–5 senior John Farmer the defensive assignment on Sellers, and it produced two quick fouls on our best player.

"I thought about taking (Sellers) out, and usually I would in that situation," said Young. "But I thought I'd see how it worked out."

St. John's got off to a quick start, taking a 13–4 lead, and had Sellers in that early foul trouble.

"I paced myself," said Sellers, who would not pick up his third foul until midway through the second half. "I tried not to be overly aggressive."

We regrouped to get back to within 14–12, but St. John's continued to push us, opening up a 24–16 lead. Another potential obstacle developed when Mike Dabney picked up his third foul six minutes before halftime.

Sellers and Dabney were the two players we always counted on in big games, but we had a talented and deep roster that included future NBA draft picks Eddie Jordan, James Bailey, and Hollis Copeland, as well as game-tested reserves like Abdel Anderson, Mark Conlin, Steve Hefele, Stan Nance, Mike Palko, Bruce Scherer, and me. With Dabney on the bench and Sellers playing cautiously on defense to avoid picking up his third foul, we would need every player on the roster to contribute.

We led by six points at the half, and I was satisfied with the score, since our top two scorers were in foul trouble. During halftime, Coach Young reminded us to keep digging in defensively and not to be afraid to double if the opportunity presented itself. He said he wanted to start the second half in our 3–2 zone ("41 defense"). He felt it might take them out of their game for a couple of minutes, which would allow us to jump on them offensively.

So much for those plans. Less than two minutes into the second half, Dabney headed to the bench with his fourth foul. That was when Hollis Copeland took over. He hit jumper after jumper and played stellar defense, helping in a big way with the rebounding as well.

Our biggest lead in the second half was 54–44 after Abdel Anderson hit one of his "Dick Barnett" jump shots. But St. John's wouldn't go away. It whittled our lead to 58–53 with 4:49 to go.

With 3:30 to play, Sellers and Smith made Madison Square Garden their personal playground. I had watched Phil take over games many times, and he did it with a scowl and a determination that embodied his no-nonsense intensity.

We had a 58–55 lead when Coach Young called time-out to make sure everyone was on the same page for the stretch run. As Young was serving up that reminder, Sellers interrupted him.

"Coach," he said, "give me the ball. I can take him." By "him," he meant Smith.

Young pretended not to hear Sellers until the best player in Rutgers history became adamant, repeating his demand for the ball a second and then a third time.

"Give me the damn ball," Sellers said, more forcefully this time.

There was no debate after that. We knew Sellers was going to get the ball. Who else would you want to have the ball with your season in the balance?

Jordan looked him in the eye and said, "I'm going to you, Phil."

Everyone knew then that the game rested with Sellers.

"We don't normally play that way," Sellers said later. "Coach really doesn't like it. But Smith had foul trouble, and I knew I could take him."

Jordan knew it was the right decision before the late drama unfolded.

"If you were in a dark alley and needed someone to fight on your side, it would be Phil," he said. "He was the guy out there. To see him take a guy like Beaver Smith, who has a really good reputation, three straight times with the game on the line—after telling the coach 'just give me the ball'—was something to see. He scored three different ways on Beaver too.

"Tom and Phil had gone at it a few times in huddles. But that time, I am out on the court with Phil, so I am on Phil's side. In the huddle with Phil there was always a back-and-forth. But that's what made Tom a great coach. He said, 'This is the time when you're right, Phil. Get it done.'"

"Someone had to take control to secure a victory," said Assistant Coach Art Perry. "Just before the whistle to return to the floor, I could see the determination in Phil's eyes. He wanted the ball and to put us on his back. Phil and Beaver were going to decide this game, and Phil won the battle when he scored the next six points to gain control of the game. He was an amazing athlete, which I had the privilege of experiencing from a front-row seat."

When we took the ball out after that time-out, Jordan delivered on his promise and got the ball to Sellers immediately. Then Sellers delivered on his promise as well.

Smith was in his defensive stance when Sellers gave him a head fake, drove to his right, and went in for an acrobatic layup to increase our lead to 60–55.

St. John's answered with a basket, but so did Sellers—again—drilling a fifteen-foot fadeaway jumper after he shook off Smith with three incredible fakes.

Again, St. John's responded with a basket. And again, Sellers did the same.

This time he drove by Smith to push our lead to 64–59 with only 1:40 remaining.

After St. John's called a time-out, Cecil Rellford cut our lead to three again. But Hollis Copeland, who would be named Most Outstanding Player of the tournament, scored on a basket that was called goaltending.

A foul shot by Smith made the score 68–64 with forty-eight seconds remaining. And that was when we went into our "5 game," which was a four-corners stall.

With twenty-two seconds to play, Rellford fouled James Bailey, who calmly sank his two foul shots for a 70–64 lead. At that point, the Rutgers fans in the evenly split crowd started chanting "We're number one!"

Rutgers won, 70–67, and Smith gave credit where it was due—to Sellers.

"When we would get it down to three, he was the man who put them back up five almost every time," said Smith. "He did it. He really did it. That is the optimal playground compliment. The dude did it. Give it to him."

Abdel Anderson, one of our two freshmen, watched Sellers' late-game sequence with star-struck admiration.

"I felt certain after that game that there was no better player I had ever played with than Phil Sellers," Anderson said. "I had never seen anybody do the things that he did during that spurt against Beaver Smith to win the game for us."

Mike Palko had seen Sellers excel for four years as his classmate, but the one-on-one confrontation with Smith was different. He recognized immediately that there was something special about it.

"It's no exaggeration," Palko said. "When we needed buckets, Phil said, 'Just give me the ball,' I never heard him verbalize it—and I am sure he said it a lot—as emphatically as he did late in that game. He was telling people that this is my neighborhood, give me the ball, Beaver Smith can't stop me, I'll get it done. And he certainly did."

After the game, while we stood at center court, surrounded by fans and our cheerleaders, it was announced that Copeland had been named Most Outstanding Player, in part because the media vote for the award was tallied with five minutes to play. But Copeland was terrific and a very deserving award winner, scoring twenty-two points on 11-of-14 shooting while grabbing ten rebounds.

"At one time, that might have bothered me if I were younger and had a good game and didn't get the award," said Sellers. "But Hollis played a great game and deserved it."

Copeland was "surprised" he was named Most Outstanding Player, adding that "Phil came through down the stretch today. He showed all of his ability."

Carnesecca paid Sellers the ultimate compliment afterward.

"Today, Sellers proved himself a clutch performer, a pro in every sense of the word," he said.

Our "reward" for the hard-earned victory was a rematch with our New Jersey rival, Princeton, a week later in Providence, as the No. 1 seed in the East Regional. We were 28–0 now, and we were certain our NCAA tournament run would take us to places no Rutgers basketball team had ever been before. It almost didn't happen though.

SECTION TWO: TEAM LEADERSHIP

Mike Dabney, Captain; Tom Young,
Head Coach; Phil Sellers, Captain

James Bailey scoring 2 of his
2034 career points

James Bailey's Sky Hook

James Bailey shows his
dominance defensively

Hollis Copeland scores two of his
1,769 career points at the "Barn"

Abdel Anderson taking his
"Dick Barnett" style jump shot

Jeff Kleinbaum scoring the 100th
point of the game as Bruce
Scherer follows the play

Abdel Anderson about to grab
a rebound at the Barn

Hollis Copeland shows his
"High Jump" form at the Barn

Abdel Anderson pouring in
two impressive points

Abdel Anderson and James Bailey
as Freshmen

Bruce Scherer, Mike Palko, Mike Dabney, Phil Sellers,
and Jeff Kleinbaum as Freshmen

Eddie Jordan scores against U.C.L.A. in the Final Four against U.C.L.A.

Art Parry (partly hidden) Tom Young, John McFadden, Joe Boylan, and Dr. Fertig (team dentist) await a game at the "Barn" to begin

Mike Dabney putting in a contested turnaround vs. Princeton at Jadwin Gym

Bruce Scherer and Mike Dabney double team Beaver Smith at Madison Square Garden

Abdel Anderson and Mark Conlin after each broke his nose in a game against the Citadel

Bruce Scherer shows off his
patented jump shot

Tom Young watches the action
in front of the bench

Mike Dabney scores on one of his
patented fast break lay ups.

Eddie Jordan takes a foul shot in
the Final Four against Michigan

Eddie Jordan scoring two of his
1,632 career points in a critical
game against Connecticut

Bruce Scherer defends against
Beaver Smith of St. Johns at
Madison Square Garden

Mike Palko about to block a shot at
Madison Square Garden

Eddie Jordan shows his classic form
at Madison Square Garden

Mike Dabney scoring two
of his 1,902 career points
on a fast break lay up

Bruce Scherer and Mike Dabney
double team Beaver Smith at
Madison Square Garden

Mark Conlin: Looking over the
defense before calling a play

Eddie Jordan scores
against Princeton

Phil Sellers soars above
everyone to block a shot as
Bruce Scherer looks on

Mike Palko slaps the ball away as
Mike Dabney and Phil Sellers
prepare to get the ball

Mike Palko shows his
defensive prowess

Mike Palko blocks another
shot for Rutgers

DESTINATION PHILADELPHIA

AFTER A REGULAR SEASON IN which we had been seriously tested five or six times (Purdue, Princeton, Manhattan, St. Bonaventure, and St. John's), everyone on our team understood the NCAA tournament would be different.

A loss during the regular season meant the end of our unbeaten record. A loss in the NCAA tournament, as we'd learned the year before against Louisville, would mean an abrupt end to our season.

So we expected the NCAA tournament games to be closer, more pressurized, and fiercely competitive, especially in what was at the time an undiluted thirty-two-team tournament.

But we never expected our first-round game against Princeton to be as excruciating and harrowing as it turned out to be—especially since we had beaten the Tigers by thirteen points in their gym the previous month.

On March 13 in Providence, Rhode Island, after more than thirty-nine minutes of some of the most agonizing basketball most of us had ever been involved in, we had a 54–53 lead and had spent nearly a minute holding the ball and trying to bleed as much time as we could off the clock.

Then, with thirty-nine seconds remaining, Mike Dabney was fouled.

Dabney had always been one of our most reliable free-throw shooters, but this time he missed the front end of a one-and-one, and

Princeton grabbed the rebound. The game suddenly became Princeton's to win or lose, since the Tigers had the final possession.

For the next thirty-five seconds Princeton passed, weaved, and worked for an opening, but none appeared.

Something that is important to note here: Armond Hill, the Ivy League Player of the Year, had fouled out with 4:37 to play, and Princeton Coach Pete Carril turned to Pete Molloy, a seldom-used reserve, to replace him.

Molloy had scored only thirty-one points all season. More importantly, he entered the game 9-for-16 from the foul line for the season and had not made a free throw since December. That proved to be significant when Eddie Jordan fouled him with four seconds remaining, sending him to the line for a one-and-one that could decide the game.

"I was guarding Pete Molloy, and the ball was moving around, and he cut backdoor," recalled Jordan, who led all Rutgers scorers with sixteen points. "I was following the ball and not realizing where he was. When the ball got back to him, I was thinking, 'Damn, I'm behind him, not in front of him.' As he drove to the basket, I reached in as he was going for his shot. I thought it was a jump ball and was doing a thumb's up. The referee didn't see it that way and called a foul on me."

As Molloy prepared for the biggest free throws of his life, Coach Young called consecutive time-outs, "just to make him think some more."

Young gave us specific instructions for any scenario; his voice was the only one heard during the huddle.

"If he makes both, call time-out," he said. "If he makes the first but not the second, get it and call time-out. If he misses the first, get the darn rebound and hold on to it for dear life."

As I told *The New York Times* afterward, I felt helpless watching everything unfold. It was terrible. I was hoping Molloy would get rattled, but Princeton had not been rattled all game long.

Mike Dabney refused to accept the possibility that our season could be over.

"We can't go out like this. We came so far, and we can't let it end like this," he said.

Jordan was close to being inconsolable after committing the foul.

"I was so upset with myself, because I was the one who fouled him," he said. "I kept replaying the moment we made contact, and I was trying to convince myself that it should have been a jump ball. I couldn't believe I did that."

Shortly after returning to the court after those consecutive time-outs, with the fate of our season in Molloy's hands, Dabney walked over to Hollis Copeland and predicted what might happen.

"Dip came over to me as we lined up for the foul shot and whispered to me, 'He doesn't look right,' " Copeland recalled. " 'I think he is going to miss it. He might even airball it, so be ready.' "

It was a prescient observation.

"After Eddie fouled Pete Molloy (and after Young called the two time-outs), I was looking at him as he went to the foul line," Dabney said. "You can tell when someone says, 'Yeah, I want to be the man, and I'm going to make this.' But his body language was more 'Do I really want to be here?'

"When the ball is released, if you play enough basketball, you can tell by the trajectory if the ball is going in or not. I could tell it was long. I knew it was going to hit the back of the rim because it was too high. I was boxing out the shooter and the ball ended up in my hands."

Despite the miss, Molloy insisted afterward that he was ready to meet the moment.

"I didn't feel any pressure," he said. "I was just thinking how great it would be if I could make both."

Molloy's free throw hit the back rim and caromed to Dabney, who went up, grabbed the rebound, and cradled it as if our life depended on it—which, of course, in the NCAA tournament, it did.

"Our whole season was flashing before our eyes as we were watching that unfold from the bench," said Mike Palko. "I was glad when Coach called a couple of time-outs to ice the shooter. I remember finding out afterward, whoever the announcer was on TV that day, asking, 'What would you do if you were Coach Carril?' And the other announcer said, 'I would take a ball out of the ball bag and have that kid practice free throws.'

"Eddie said it was a stupid foul on his part, but if he didn't foul him, maybe he dishes it off for a layup."

What made our second win of the season over Princeton even more satisfying was that we did not react a month earlier after the first victory when Carril made a disparaging remark about us. Asked if he would like to have a rematch in the NCAA tournament, Carril said, "I'd like to see how they would do against us in a book-reading contest."

Obviously, that did not go over well in our locker room, but we held our tongues. Our response was simply another win over the Tigers.

As for the lead-up to Molloy's free-throw moment, it was mostly yawn-inducing basketball, all because of Princeton's deliberate style of play.

Princeton held two leads during the first half, 16–14 and 18–16. There was one tie as well—20–20 with 7:10 left in the first half. Then we ran off eight straight points—baskets by Sellers, Jordan, Abdel Anderson, and Copeland—in a three-minute span. That eventually left us with a 33–25 halftime lead.

We took a ten-point lead at the outset of the second half when Copeland tapped in a miss, and we still led by ten, 39–29, with 17:20 to play.

That was when Princeton began chipping away at our advantage. Sellers was a little off, hitting only three of fifteen shots for the game, with Dabney shooting 5-for-14. We were getting good shots; they just weren't falling.

Princeton took advantage of our offensive struggles to outscore us 10–2 as Hill, Barnes Hauptfuhrer, Frank Sowinski, and Bob Slaughter brought the Tigers back. With twelve minutes to play, and with our lead at 41–39, Dabney led a mini-charge, making a three-point play as we outscored the Tigers during a 7–2 spurt.

To the surprise of no one, Princeton fought back again to get within 50–47 with 5:09 remaining. We eventually had a 54–51 lead, but it was clear we were out of sorts on offense, since we didn't score over the final 4:37. When we reached fifty-four—our lowest point total of the season—we did not score again.

After Bill Omeltchenko made it 54–51, Hauptfuhrer hit a jump shot from the top of the key with less than a minute to play to make the score 54–53.

Molloy's big moment was next.

"I was very anxious, but I knew that Molloy hadn't taken many foul shots, and then Coach froze him by calling two time-outs in a row," said Mark Conlin.

Molloy said afterward that he felt confident heading to the foul line, despite having attempted only sixteen foul shots all season.

"I thought the foul shot was good when I let it go," he said after the game. "The time-outs didn't bother me. None of the Rutgers players said anything before I shot. Nobody tried to psyche me out. I thought it was going to be good."

Pete Carril was his typical philosophical self.

"We had everything going for us with four seconds left," he said. "We came so close. We could've beaten Rutgers."

As Princeton made what was likely a longer-than-usual bus ride back home from Providence, we immediately turned our focus to what was next: the East Regionals in Greensboro, North Carolina.

With our travel plans determined, we headed home for a couple of days of classes, practice, and rest (thank goodness). Connecticut, a team we had beaten 96–83 in December despite Tony Hanson giving us fits with a twenty-eight-point performance, was the next threat to our 29–0 season.

As we prepared for UConn, we were pleased to learn that our cheerleaders would be going to North Carolina with us. Having them and our energizing pep band, led by Dr. Scott Whitener, with us was welcome news, because they were always part of our routine and they supported us with spirit and pride.

The cheerleading squad, featuring seven men and three women, most of them from New Jersey, had a number of terrific performers. Cramer was a senior from Martinsville; Debbie Zern hailed from Wyckoff; and Cathy Koch came from Millstone. Those three were joined by Jeff Trefecante from Nutley; Lou Fusilli from Wyckoff; Steve Fittante of Middletown; and Dwayne Yanmasaki from Bridgeton.

In my mind, our pep band was as good as there was in college basketball.

That year was also an election year, something that became part of our North Carolina experience. When we arrived in Greensboro, there was a large sign on our hotel that read "Welcome, Rutgers."

Later that day, the sign was taken down and replaced by a sign that said, "Welcome, Ronald Reagan." Reagan, who would be elected president in 1980, was in Greensboro campaigning for the Republican presidential nomination against President Gerald Ford. Reagan stayed in our hotel along with some movie stars who supported him. (Reagan was an actor and the president of the Screen Actors Guild before he turned to politics.)

One of the celebrities campaigning with Reagan was Jimmy Stewart, one of the finest actors ever to grace Hollywood and a real favorite of my mom and dad.

The morning before our game against Connecticut, I was in my hotel room when the phone rang. It was Assistant Coach Joe Boylan.

"Jeff, do you know Jimmy Stewart, the actor?" he asked.

"Yes, of course," I replied.

"Good. Come on down to the lobby in five minutes, because you and Mike Palko are going to take a picture with him."

I practically sprinted to the lobby, where Stewart was signing autographs and posing for photos. Coach Boylan brought Mike and me over to him, and we chatted for a minute or two.

"You guys are having quite a season," said Stewart.

"We still have a way to go," replied Palko.

With that, we stuck a Rutgers pin on him and took several pictures that were sent to the national media outlets. When my parents and family saw that picture of me with Jimmy Stewart, they were ecstatic.

Sports broadcaster Bruce Beck of WNBC-TV in New York, who grew up a Rutgers fan in large part because of his father, made the trip to North Carolina from New Jersey with his family. Beck's dad, Felix Beck, was a Rutgers graduate who served for seventeen years on the school's Board of Governors and Board of Trustees.

"We had a bumper sticker that read 'Rutgers Rampage,' " Beck recalled. "That was the big thing at the time. We had it on the back of my dad's car, and as we were driving through Maryland, we got pulled over for speeding. My dad talked his way out of the ticket, but when we got to the next stop, we saw that the cop had ripped off the Rutgers Rampage bumper sticker."

Respect from opposing coaches came much more easily.

On the day we played Connecticut, its coach, Dee Rowe, was generous with his praise of our team.

"I could easily be a Rutgers fan," said Rowe. "They are so much fun to watch. They are just not fun to play."

The welcome news for us, after going through the basketball torture chamber of Princeton, was that Connecticut liked to run.

"We really don't have much of a choice," said Rowe. "We've played a running game all season, and this isn't the time to change. We might try to slow the tempo a bit, but we're not going to play a slowdown. It wouldn't work."

The game turned out to be similar to our first meeting with Connecticut. Hanson was a dominant force again, with twenty-three points and nine rebounds despite sitting out a long stretch with foul trouble. He just needed additional support beyond a twenty-four-point performance by Al Weston.

Sellers's shooting was off for the second straight game (4-for-13 for eight points), but our depth more than made up for his struggles. Anderson came off the bench to score nineteen points and grab eleven rebounds, and our outstanding guard tandem of Jordan and Dabney had eighteen points apiece. Steve Hefele, playing a major role off the bench, had one of his best games of the year, shooting 7-for-9 for fourteen points to go along with seven rebounds.

Our defense, our quickness, and our depth once again carried the day, and we left the arena one step closer to the Final Four with a 93–79 victory.

To be honest, we were all surprised that our road to the Final Four did not include a game against Tennessee, which had been ranked

No. 9 in the Associated Press Top 20 poll heading into the NCAA tournament.

The Volunteers were a terrific team with two high-profile future NBA stars in Bernard King and Ernie Grunfeld, a high-scoring duo known as "The Ernie and Bernie Show."

Grunfeld averaged 25.3 points that season; King averaged 25.2 points and thirteen rebounds.

I had gotten to know Grunfeld because we were both from Queens and we played in All-Star games together. He became quite a legend back home, and he would not only go on to have a solid NBA career as a player, but he became general manager of the Knicks and Bucks before becoming president of the Washington Wizards during a long and distinguished career as an NBA executive.

King, of course, had an outstanding fourteen-year career in the NBA that led to his induction into the Basketball Hall of Fame in 2013.

But on the same day we squeaked by Princeton, Tennessee fell victim in a stunning 81–75 loss to unranked Virginia Military Institute. VMI followed that upset win by defeating No. 17-ranked DePaul, 71–66, in overtime.

To be honest, the realization had not yet hit us that we were just a win over VMI away from going to the Final Four. Most of us didn't even know where VMI was located (it's in Lexington, Virginia).

Coach Young had watched VMI beat DePaul (he sent us back to our hotel to rest) and was impressed.

"What surprised me is that they fast break," he said. "They look for it. Not too many teams have really run against us this year, or have tried to. But I expect them to try it, and it could hurt us."

They were not a big team heightwise, but they were physically strong.

"We don't have a kid who is 6–10 that we give him the ball and have him go to the hole with it," Bill Blair, VMI's coach, said before our game.

What they did have was a disciplined team (as military teams often are) that moved the ball around until they got a good shooting opportunity from fifteen to eighteen feet, and then they shot with consistency.

Ron Carter (17.9 points per game) and Will Bynum (15.5 ppg) were their scoring leaders. As a team, VMI shot an impressive 51.1 percent.

We prepared as we always did at this time of year. We watched several films of VMI games and discussed how we would play them and what the matchups would be. We went over what we wanted to do defensively and then took the floor for a short practice the day before the game.

Coach Young did not believe in hard, intense practices at this time of year. We all knew what we needed to do, and we were in shape and ready to go. Just some fine tuning was all he wanted.

When we took the floor against VMI, we were probably a little too eager. The early part of the game was sluggish, with VMI taking a 27–26 lead and no doubt thinking it was going to pull off another upset of a ranked opponent.

That was when we showed them what a Rutgers was (that's a reference to what some people from other parts of the country said about us). We led 48–34 at the half, and we felt we were solidly in command.

But VMI didn't chalk up those upset wins over Tennessee and DePaul on a fluke. They were a solid team with quality players. They cut our 62–41 lead to 68–58 with 8:26 to go.

VMI Coach Blair decided to switch from a zone defense to man-to-man, because we had slowed things down and they needed points quickly. But it didn't work. With Jordan running our offense and Dabney showing his senior leadership, we took control again down the stretch and won 91–75.

Dabney and Jordan each had twenty-three points, Sellers had sixteen, and Copeland and Anderson each had eight. I had one point. Alas, it was not the hundredth, since we didn't reach that number.

There was a moment when the game ended that we all let out a tremendous sigh of relief. It didn't sink in until later, but we went around hugging each other as many of our supporters paraded around the court with a pennant of every team we'd beaten hanging on a pole. Now that we were 31–0, it was a long pole.

I hugged Sellers; he was quiet and looked drained. It made me think back to the very first time I played with him at Five-Star Basketball

Camp, when he told me I'd better pass him the ball anytime I was on the court with him.

He deserved that introspective moment. Actually, we all did. We had accomplished something very few athletes get to experience.

I thought back to when I chose to play basketball for Rutgers over a possible career in baseball, and I knew at that moment that I had made the right choice. We were going to the Final Four. There were only four teams left, and we were one of them. One of the other teams was Indiana. It remains the last time two unbeaten teams reached the Final Four.

The sense of accomplishment and the satisfaction I felt—that all of us felt—was unlike anything I'd ever experienced.

Rutgers, at 31–0, was going to the Final Four. Let that sink in, and savor it for a while.

THE FINAL FOUR

NOTHING COULD HAVE PREPARED US for the week leading up to the Final Four. Everything was magnified, and it took every ounce of discipline we had to keep our focus on the game. The media crush was like nothing I had ever experienced, with a steady stream of interviews and questions, compounded by our fans' excitement and eagerness to share the moment with us.

This also was when the Final Four was really taking off as a major sporting event; the seismic shift would occur even more three years later, in 1979, when Larry Bird and Magic Johnson would go head-to-head in the game that would change everything about college basketball.

We were acutely aware of what most of the country—outside of our circle—was thinking with Indiana, UCLA, Michigan, and Rutgers in the Final Four.

"I remember being in the hotel room with Mark Conlin and saying, 'Michigan, Indiana, UCLA, and Rutgers. Which one is the sore thumb in that group?' " said Steve Hefele. "All of a sudden we were in the Final Four with three bluebloods."

The one thing that kept things somewhat normal for us was our preparation for Michigan. We found out they were our opponent in the March 27 semifinal the same night they learned we were theirs. The winner of our game would meet the winner of the other semifinal, between Indiana and UCLA, in the national championship game on Monday night, March 29, at The Spectrum in Philadelphia.

I kept thinking about those words: *national championship game*. My entire life, I followed sports. My father and I would watch every sport and would always look forward to teams reaching the pinnacle of their sport, whether it was the Super Bowl, World Series, Stanley Cup Finals, or the NBA Finals.

Now I was part of that. It's truly difficult to put into words the impact that had on me.

In a media session, Coach Young said the favorite was the other unbeaten team, No.1-ranked Indiana, with the caveat that "Any one of the Final Four teams has a chance to win it."

"It takes your best effort of the year to make it out of the Final Four alive," Young added. "Right now, we are playing as well as we have been playing all year, but we can't afford a letdown."

Our preparation started with watching film, seeing how Michigan played and what it liked to do offensively and defensively, followed by an hour and a half of practice.

It was apparent immediately that Michigan had impressive team speed and liked to overplay passes to upset its opponents' offenses. To that end, Coach Young devised three plays we would run at the start of the game. To my knowledge, we had never "scripted" plays before, but this time it made perfect sense.

The first time we had the ball on offense; the plan was for Eddie Jordan to bring up the ball on the right side of the court. Phil Sellers would line up on the block on that same side, and as Jordan dribbled toward him, Sellers would pop out to the wing and then go backdoor.

The second designed play was similar, except this time Jordan would go to the left side, and Mike Dabney would set up on the block, pop out, and then go backdoor.

The third scripted play had Jordan bringing the ball up on the sideline again, but this time with James Bailey starting on the foul line before cutting to the top of the key. Bailey would then reverse and go backdoor.

Three trips down the court, three back doors. That was the plan. If only it were that simple.

Here is the problem with scripted plays: As well-executed as they are in practice, there's no way to account for how an opponent will respond and try to disrupt things.

On the Monday before the Final Four weekend, the City Council of New Brunswick organized a lunchtime parade and rally ending at the steps of city hall. One of the city council members, Ed "Cazzie" Carman, promoted the event heavily. He was an ardent Rutgers supporter and someone we got to know quite well. He and his brother, Herb, were the type of people who would do anything for you.

On the day of the parade, I was taken aback. When we showed up at city hall, we were greeted by a crowd estimated at between ten and twelve thousand supporters. That was really remarkable, considering our school was out on spring break.

The rally was exhilarating; it gave us a sense of what lay ahead when we set off for Philadelphia later in the week. After the rally, Bruce Scherer and I went back to our apartment on Easton Avenue. Unbeknown to us, some fans followed us, and they started yelling for us in front of the apartment building.

When I heard it, I went to the window and saw nearly two dozen people, mostly girls, calling for us. It felt like we were mini celebrities.

We were able to avoid them by slipping out the back door of our apartment to head to the Barn for practice.

Since the semifinal game against Michigan was on Saturday, we left after practice on Thursday and bused to Philadelphia. It was comforting to see and hear the guys up to their usual bus antics, because it kept things normal.

Once we arrived, it was apparent that the Final Four was a big deal to the people in Philadelphia too. Signs about the games were everywhere, and sportscasters talked about it on every nightly news show. In our hotel, we found ourselves surrounded by autograph seekers.

"If there was a time for me to say and feel like we've arrived, it was when we got to Philadelphia and you saw all of the media," said Bailey. "That was real national attention, and it dawned on you that we're the only four teams left. That was the time it really hit me what we had accomplished."

One thing I noticed right away that made this much different from other games had nothing to do with our opponent. We saw Michigan as another opponent, and we were highly confident. But all the other distractions creeped into our preparation. It became obvious to all of us that this was a national event.

Bailey and Abdel Anderson, our two freshmen, tried to make sense of it all.

"I don't think anybody realized that we were two eighteen-year-old freshmen, just nine months from playing in high school, and we're suddenly being placed in this huge event," said Bailey. "It was definitely next-level, and I must say, there were times that the scrutiny became overwhelming."

Each team was allowed one hour on the court on Friday, the day before the semifinals, for an open practice session that fans could attend for free. The schedule was UCLA, Rutgers, Indiana, and Michigan. When we arrived at The Spectrum for our practice session, we were immediately ushered into our locker room. As we were walking in, it seemed like there was a large crowd on hand to watch UCLA, the defending national champion.

When it was our turn, I was a bit stunned by what I saw. There were more than ten thousand people there, just to watch us go through an informal practice.

On the day of the game, I spent more than two hours trying to arrange tickets for family and friends. That was not something I wanted to do, but one good thing was that it took up time and kept my mind off the game.

When we arrived for our game, we were pretty loose and quietly confident, I thought. When we left the locker room and took the court, we were greeted by a thunderous ovation. Our pep band played our fight song, and we went through our "single exchange" warm-up and then our layup line. It was comforting to hear our pep band and see our cheerleaders doing their thing too.

One thing struck me while we were warming up: Since we were the first game of the doubleheader, the game didn't go live on NBC until fifteen minutes before tipoff. Just about at that time, while we were in our layup line, the public address announcer could be heard above the buzz in the arena.

"In a few minutes," he announced, "we will be joined by over forty million people who will be watching this game. So when we say so, let's give the audience around the world a big Philadelphia welcome."

It made me think about how we were coming from a gym that held 2,800 and local TV broadcasting to an arena that seated 18,168, with forty million watching on TV.

Before getting into the Michigan game, I want you to know how difficult it was for me for a very long time to relive the outcome. I was devastated after we lost to Michigan. I was, and always will be, very proud of my teammates, but my heart sank that night. I was distraught. I felt so bad for everyone associated with Rutgers, and I was at a complete loss with how to deal with it.

Until recently, nearly fifty years later, I did not watch any of the film of the game, and I'm generally reluctant even to discuss it. It's easy to suggest that I should be over it a half-century later, but it wasn't until a recent conversation with Mark Conlin that I made my peace with what happened.

"Jeff, I was upset after the game, of course," Conlin told me. "But I was able to recover from that pretty quickly, because I realized how much we did for ourselves, for the university, and for the wonderful people who cheered for us night in and night out.

"We did something that no Rutgers team has ever done, and we have lived with that most of our lives. Maybe it didn't end like we had hoped, but I wouldn't trade what we did for anything. Would you?"

When I left Conlin's house that day, I drove home and finally watched the tape of the game. It was not pleasant to sit through, but I realized that was us out there, playing in the Final Four, one game away from the national championship, and we had galvanized support throughout New Jersey as few sports teams ever have.

With my memory refreshed from watching the film, I can say that both teams started with Final Four jitters.

We ran our "scripted" plays at the start of the game perfectly, with just one problem: We missed layups on the first two plays, and Bailey was fouled on his backdoor attempt, making one of his two free throws. That alone probably should have been a warning sign.

The opening 8:30 was fairly even, with Michigan leading 11–10. Then the Wolverines went on a 10–2 run that gave them some breathing room at 21–12.

As we got closer to the end of the first half, we were doing what we could to stay within reach, but Michigan kept building its lead. It was ahead, 46–29, at halftime.

Any attempt to stage a comeback was thwarted because our shooting betrayed us.

We shot just 39 percent for the game, compared to 47.7 percent for the season; our star upperclassmen—Sellers, Dabney, and Jordan—were a combined 16-for-51 from the floor.

"Michigan punched us in the face that game," said Hollis Copeland. "When you get punched in the face, you have to punch back immediately. I think we started feeling our jaws before we punched back."

In the locker room at halftime, we were struggling to sort out what had just happened.

"I remember being in the locker room at halftime and looking around and seeing how stunned everyone was," said Hefele. "For thirty-one games, we had never felt that. It was rough."

The second half went more as everyone (or at least we) thought the game would go all along. Both teams had their moments, but we just couldn't get one of our patented runs together to cut into Michigan's lead. We weren't shooting well, but Michigan couldn't completely shake us.

With just under eleven minutes to play, we had pulled within nine points. But from that point on, Michigan would respond each time we scored, with John Robinson (twenty points and sixteen rebounds), Phil Hubbard (sixteen points and thirteen rebounds), and lightning-quick Ricky Green (sixteen points, six assists) always ready to keep the Wolverines in control.

They were a quality team, and their players deserved that 86–70 win. But that didn't make the outcome any easier to accept.

Coach Young was noticeably upset after the game, and some of that raw emotion spilled into his postgame comments to the media.

"We stunk the place out," said Young. "To me, it's a shame for Rutgers, a shame for Eastern basketball. Don't get me wrong; Michigan is a good team. But we played teams that were as quick and aggressive."

A little later, after he had time to collect his thoughts and calm down, Young gave full credit to Michigan, though he added, "We picked the wrong night to have a bad game."

Copeland was one of our few players who played to his usual standards, scoring fifteen points to go along with seven rebounds, three steals, and one block.

We had always been able to overcome an off-day from one or, at times, even two of our stars. But Sellers, Dabney, and Jordan all struggling at the same time proved to be too much.

"It shocked me because Dip, Phil, and Eddie did not have good games," said Copeland. "I'm not blaming them, but it was uncharacteristic for all of them to be off in the same game. It was just one of those things."

Afterward, Jordan suggested that being a first-time Final Four team may have factored into our performance.

"I think they were more familiar with that type of atmosphere," Jordan said. "We played at Madison Square Garden, but that was more like a home away from home for us. Then we get to the Final Four, and things were considerably next-level.

"Cameras were everywhere, and time-outs took forever. But credit Michigan. They were fast. They were aggressive. They attacked. They were just better than we were that night."

Mike Dabney was upset for several reasons. The biggest one was that we lost the game, but he had a concern that a few people talked about. He suspected Michigan had some inside knowledge about the basketballs that were used.

"I have said this before," said Dabney. "The ball they used for our game was too slippery, and it was because they wanted a nice, fresh, bright ball for national TV. I looked over to the Michigan bench and I saw that they had rosin, and "sticky pads" for their sneakers too. They kept putting their hands in the rosin for a better grip.

"If you look at the first pass that came to me, it slipped right through my fingers. I had great hands, Jerry Rice-type hands. I didn't fumble the ball. But the ball was so slippery, and we didn't have any rosin. I went over to Coach Young and said, 'The ball is really slippery. Can we get another ball?' But that was not going to happen."

To Dabney, it all seemed a little suspicious.

"Here's the thing," he said. "Why did they have rosin? How did they know to have rosin on their bench?"

Palko started to share Dabney's concerns after they talked.

"I didn't notice anything about the rosin at the time, but I did think that the ball was extremely slippery," he said. "I saw the ball slipping out of Phil's hands on one layup and doing the same thing coming out of Mike's hands. It started to make sense when Mike told me about the rosin bag. I didn't even know what a rosin bag was. It turns out those teams with experience had all sorts of things to help them. They also had tack mats for their shoes. We didn't have that.

"We were throwing off-target passes and fumbling the ball, and I was thinking, 'What's going on here?' We did things that were so out of character that there had to be a reason. It's not something to blame, but it's an observation that has a lot of implications behind it."

Everyone on our team seemed to have a reason or an explanation for what happened. Assistant Coach John McFadden's assessment was blunt:

"We got punked," he said. "Physically, they were better. We had some stars in our eyes. Waymon Britt was as much a stud as Phil was, just not quite as tall. Phil Hubbard was much better than James Bailey because he was older and stronger. Ricky Greene was as quick if not quicker than Eddie Jordan. For the first time all year we played a team that was physically superior to us. Stronger and just as quick and more experienced in those situations.

"When you play a game like that, if you go down the wrong road, sometimes it is very difficult to get back on the right one. I think one of the contributing factors to that is you suddenly don't have your swagger. You lose some confidence and then you are trying too hard. If things are not going your way, it becomes very difficult to trust your offense and your defense. Then it's easy to hit the panic button, get out of character a little, and then bad goes to worse. Being down as much as we were at halftime, that was not indicative of the talent level of the two teams, I didn't think.

"When you add to that the physical aspect, that we could not dictate to them physically, we couldn't turn them over, and Phil couldn't go in and have his way inside, I think that was a punch to the face. I think they were just much more comfortable going into that game, having been battle-tested more than we were."

After the game, when we left the arena, most of us just wanted a quiet night to be with our thoughts. But the Rutgers Athletic Department was having a reception in our honor back at the hotel. It had been organized days before the game and was supposed to be a kind of celebration. Since we lost, it was the last thing any of us wanted to go to.

But if we didn't go, it would seem like we didn't care about all the people who traveled to see us, so of course we all went. The mood in the banquet room was somber, similar to the feeling when losing political candidates have to concede elections in front of their supporters. I was glad to see my parents, of course, but nobody quite knew what to say to any of us, and we had very little to say back.

On top of that, we had one more game to play: the consolation game Monday night against UCLA, which lost 66–51 to Indiana in the other semifinal.

I can't think of anything worse than playing in the consolation game of the Final Four. It wasn't until six years later, in time for the 1981 Final Four, that the NCAA eliminated the game.

When you take the court for a semifinal game, you are totally focused on beating your opponent and getting to the final. Then, in a matter of three hours, all of that disappears, and you are left totally demoralized and dejected.

When Coach Young called a practice on Sunday for the consolation game, it took us a while to regain our focus. The driving force in helping us get energized in practice, preparing for the game, and having to deal with the media again, was pride.

"We have a proud bunch of kids, and we'll be ready to play UCLA," Young said the morning of the game.

"After what happened on Saturday, we felt we had something to prove," Dabney said.

I grew up watching UCLA dominate college basketball, winning ten national titles between 1964 and 1975, first with Kareem Abdul-Jabbar (who was called Lew Alcindor then), and then with Bill Walton. The idea of playing them was unlike facing any other team. They had a star-studded lineup too, with many of the same players who led them to the national title the year before: six-foot-eleven Richard Washington, six-foot-nine David Greenwood, seven-foot-two Ralph Drollinger, six-foot-seven Marques Johnson, and six-foot-three Andre McCarter. We averaged just under six-foot-seven across our starting frontcourt, so the Bruins's height advantage would be nearly impossible to overcome.

The game was a good one. The score was 15–15 after eight minutes, and it was tied again two minutes later. But UCLA opened up a 38–27 lead with two minutes to go before Steve Hefele and Hollis Copeland each had steals that led to baskets, followed by Sellers tapping in a basket to close the gap to 42–40.

Then UCLA went on a spurt and built a 57–49 lead at the half.

In the locker room, we reminded each other to continue to work hard, if only to show appreciation to our loyal fans.

With eleven minutes left in the second half, we took a 74–73 lead and fought back and forth with the defending champions. With 5:30 to play, we tied the score at 81–81, but UCLA closed out the game with a flourish. The final score was 106–92, although the game was much closer than the score indicated.

That was it. No banners, no crowds mobbing us on the court. Just a two-game losing streak to end the best season in Rutgers basketball history. After we shook hands with the UCLA players and headed back to our locker room, I was aware that I was walking off the court for the last time in a Rutgers uniform, and that I would never play a college basketball game again.

I thought back to my very first game as a freshman, against John Thompson's Georgetown team, and how wonderful it was to play at the Barn. Since that day, I had played in some of the finest arenas in college basketball, and I had seen some of the most beautiful sights our country has to offer.

More importantly, I played with eleven wonderful teammates and four great coaches, and I had the time of my life. It was all worth it. And let's be realistic: 31–2 is something to be proud of, no matter how it ended.

BACK TO NEW BRUNSWICK— AND REALITY

BOARDING THE BUS BACK TO New Brunswick the next morning took all the resolve I could muster. Still mourning the losses to Michigan—which fell to Indiana, 86–68, in the championship game—and UCLA, I walked by people with hardly a word of acknowledgment, and I did not say anything to my teammates.

At the time, I couldn't understand why I was feeling so melancholy. We had just completed the greatest season in Rutgers basketball history and had accomplished something very few teams—or players—have a chance to experience. But to me, none of that mattered. I sat down in my usual seat on the bus, put a towel over my head, and tried to take a nap, even though I knew it would be a futile effort.

I tried to distract myself, so I made a mental note to contact the Rutgers baseball coach, Matt Bolger, when we got back, to let him know I was done with basketball and could be on the baseball field as soon as he wanted me. I was secretly hoping he would tell me to take a couple of days off to recuperate and recover, but I wasn't certain he would agree to that. The baseball season had started three days before—on the day we played Michigan—and I was the captain of the team.

Two days after our consolation game against UCLA, I had a baseball game to play. We were facing Columbia at home.

On that bus ride back to Rutgers, which felt like it took forever, I knew we wouldn't have to worry about forcing smiles for people when we got home, because I had convinced myself that no one would be waiting for us there. Not after what happened at the Final Four. Alone with my thoughts, I tried to rationalize what it was that was making me so depressed. It wasn't just losing; it was losing the way we did against Michigan, and how I felt we let so many people down, and how disappointed they must be in us right now.

I kept thinking about how much time, effort, and incredible enthusiasm the people on campus, in New Brunswick, and throughout the State of New Jersey put in while supporting us throughout an incredible journey that ended the way we did not want it to end. I felt that our team and coaches had formed a bond with our fans, and I was struggling to come to grips with how we'd let them down.

I wasn't the only one feeling despondent. Mike Dabney was dejected, as well. Slumping in his seat, he said in a low voice that he felt "I had let people down."

Bruce Scherer was trying to sort through his feelings, knowing his basketball days, like mine, were over.

"The hardest part for me was seeing the disappointment and sadness in the faces of the longtime alumni and fans who were totally immersed in what we were doing during the regular season and came to see us after the games in Philadelphia," he recalled. "I felt that we had totally let them down."

I remember Stan Nance saying he felt numb.

"I totally expected us to get to the championship game," he said. "And when we didn't make it, my heart sank. I thought that we let our fans down."

When we finally arrived in New Brunswick, Louie, our bus driver, turned down College Avenue toward the Barn. There would be no need to sneak around the back and avoid the crush of our fans, I thought. I was certain our supporters weren't going to be there waiting for us.

As we passed Scott Hall and got close to Tinsley Hall, we noticed people lining the streets. Then, as we passed the student center next to the gym, there were hundreds of people cheering for us and carrying signs. One read, "You are still our Heroes." Another read, "We Love you."

Almost immediately, the mood on the bus changed, and we started feeling better about everything for the first time since the tipoff against Michigan on Saturday night. People were cheering and smiling and letting us know that what we did was truly special—for us and for them—and couldn't be taken away.

"I was pretty down after the Final Four and I thought that we had let the entire student body down," said Steve Hefele. "Then, when I saw that crowd waiting for us along College Avenue, I started to think that the bond between the fans and the players was as strong as it could be.

"What we did will stay in the minds of everyone involved for probably the rest of everyone's lives."

Hefele was spot on. To this day I still feel a closeness with the people who were at Rutgers when we returned from Philly. And when someone brings up what our team accomplished, it feels like I am talking to a family member or a close friend.

I talked to Eddie Jordan about his feelings after the losses had settled in. His take was extremely positive as well.

"Obviously, we were disappointed, but we knew we had accomplished something extra special," he said. "We played a style of basketball that would be extremely hard to copy. Probably, and more importantly, we put Rutgers on the major college basketball map. That, I think, will always mean a lot to us."

Several of the key players would be back next season, including Jordan, Hollis Copeland, Steve Hefele, Mark Conlin, Abdel Anderson, James Bailey and Stan Nance. They were determined to use our season as something both to learn from and build on.

"Two losses were a bad experience, but we'll learn from it," said Copeland. "We'll learn from what has gone down. The weekend in Philadelphia has definitely been beneficial. I hope the club has benefited as much as I have. I hope the team learned a lot of things and that our future will be much brighter."

When most teams come to the end of a season, there is a realization that the time together as a unit has come to an end. But that could not have been further from the truth for the 1975–76 Rutgers men's basketball team.

Our schedule of events for the next few months (and years) actually kept most of us together, and it allowed us to distance ourselves further from what happened in Philadelphia, which benefited everyone on the team. The State of New Jersey wanted to honor us for all that we had achieved for the people of the state, and Governor Brendan Byrne invited us to Drumthwacket, the governor's official residence in Princeton (of all places), for dinner and celebration.

Even though I was fully committed now to baseball, I was excited for the opportunity, because it was a chance to be around my basketball teammates again. Scherer and I invited the guys to our apartment for some refreshments a couple of hours before we were to leave for Princeton. We toasted each other and our fans.

When we arrived at the governor's mansion, Scherer, Conlin, Hefele, and I were in celebratory moods. When I went inside, I was taken aback by Drumthwacket's splendor. My teammates and I were seated at two large round tables that sat six, and we certainly were having a good time. Just before the speeches got underway, Scherer said he would get beers for some of us. As the speeches started, I noticed him coming back, holding four open cans of beer. I watched with curiosity, since he had to navigate three rather large steps while holding four beers.

Just as he reached the steps, and right on cue as the governor started to speak, Scherer tripped and landed face-down. His response to our uproarious laughter was to hold up the four beer cans in those big hands of his, proudly showing everyone he hadn't spilled a drop. Now that's a man who can hold his beer.

The rest of the evening was pleasant enough, and we returned home with no further incidents.

It had been announced prior to the end of the season that Rutgers had accepted an invitation to play in an international tournament in Florence and Venice. The trip to Italy was scheduled for April 18 to 25 and would include teams from Puerto Rico, Italy, and Cuba. Everyone was excited about the opportunity, in large part because it would give us a chance to play more games together.

I had one problem, though. I was playing for the Rutgers baseball team, and I was also a captain.

I spoke to my parents about the situation, and their response was that I might never have another chance to go to Italy (especially for free). I spoke to Coach Bolger and Coach Young, and they decided that it had to be my decision. Fred Gruninger, the athletic director, also weighed in.

"We paid for you to go to Italy, Jeff," Gruninger said. "You need to go with the basketball team."

For me, it was not a difficult decision, despite what others were saying. How could I call myself a captain and abruptly leave the team I was playing for and miss four games in the middle of the season? I eventually told Coach Young that I had an obligation to my baseball teammates and that I would not be making the basketball trip.

I never second-guessed myself on the decision, though I did wonder if the fates were trying to tell me something. In my first baseball game after the basketball team departed for Italy, I hurt my knee sliding into second base and missed three of the games I would have missed had I gone on the trip.

Whether I went with the basketball team or stayed home to play baseball, meal money on all road trips was the same, even after the season. We received five dollars for breakfast, eight dollars for lunch, and fifteen dollars for dinner, since our scholarships included all meals. During the season, some of us saved money by eating at the hotel where we were staying on the road and then charging our meals to the rooms we were in. The university then paid for it. Not exactly ethical, but we were all broke college kids at the time.

There was still some unfinished basketball business in the weeks leading up to the Italy trip. The guys on the team had gotten used to life without the basketball routine we had followed since October 15, and we were far enough removed from the Final Four that we were looking forward to our basketball team dinner. That event usually drew a large crowd, but this year they actually had to turn some people away.

Dr. Edward Bloustein, the president of the university, invited the players, coaches, and their wives to a pre-dinner reception at his house, which was about seventy-five yards beyond the left field fence of the baseball field. It just so happened that we had a baseball game at home that day at four p.m. I knew I would miss some time at the reception at Dr. Bloustein's, but I had it worked out in my head that I would be done in time to get to the dinner.

In the seventh inning of the game, I came to bat with runners on first and second and our team trailing 3–1. Just as I stepped to the plate, I started to hear a group of people on the outside of the left field fence calling my name. I looked out, and sure enough, my basketball team-mates were chanting my name and almost pleading with me to call my shot. Dressed in their suits, they had left the reception, made the short walk over to the baseball field, and pressed against the outfield fence.

I was trying to hide my embarrassment, but the more I ignored them, the louder they got. The count went to 2–1, and, sure enough, the pitcher threw a ball my mother could have hit. I lined it over the right field fence, and we eventually won the game.

When I arrived at the dinner, the guys were all over me, not real-izing that the pitcher threw a lousy pitch. No matter, I knew I could milk that story for many years—and I have.

Most of my basketball teammates spoke at the dinner, reflecting on the journey we'd gone through together.

"I've been fortunate to experience the 'big time' early," said fresh-man James Bailey. "I've matured both mentally and physically. We have really had a great season, the best in the history of Rutgers."

When Phil Sellers got up to speak, he was passionate about the incredible ride he had just been on with his teammates.

"We have accomplished a lot," he said. "We were undefeated coming to Philadelphia. You can't do much better than that. I had a good year and broke some all-time records, and Dip (Mike Dabney) had an excellent year too. Ed Jordan went over the one-thousand-point mark for his career. We won our first Christmas tournament and our first NCAA tournament game. And we finished off by playing UCLA. It's a nice way to go out."

Coach Young spoke last, and he focused on both the recent past and Rutgers's future.

"We're building our program, and that takes time," he said. "We will continue to build and play better and better teams."

As the basketball team prepared for its trip to Italy, I had mixed emotions. I wanted to be with those guys, because we had truly bonded into twelve brothers and I wanted to enjoy some more time with them. But I felt I had made the correct decision. I made a commitment to my baseball teammates, and I was determined to stick to it.

When they returned from Italy, I heard all the stories about the great time they had during the eight days they were there. They did a lot of sightseeing and played well on the trip, winning two of three games.

But some of them apparently missed my adult leadership. (Just kidding; I would have been right there with them.) Conlin revealed that he and three teammates had nearly gotten themselves and some pedestrians killed.

Four of them had rented Vespa scooters, which were electric and went very fast. Scherer, Conlin, Hefele, and Palko decided that since they knew how to ride bikes, they could certainly ride scooters. So much for that idea.

Conlin told everyone that he knew what he was doing and started his scooter. As soon as he released the brake, his scooter started making circles and doing wheelies, and it finally crashed into a fence where five pedestrians were standing. Nobody got hurt, but I am sure the Italian people thought we had a strange concept of humor. The guys decided to drive very slowly from that point on.

I was also told that several guys participated in "friendly" card games when they couldn't leave the hotel. That was something we did often on road trips, along with going to the movies and doing a little shopping for our parents and ourselves.

On our team, the king of the card games was Stan Nance. He always seemed to win at his favorite game, blackjack. One night, the guys stayed up until two a.m., with the next day's practice drawing closer with every hand. Nance had beaten everyone, especially a player who requested anonymity for this story to be told. He was upset when Nance got up to get some sleep and demanded that he continue playing.

"What, I can't go to sleep until I lose everything I won?" yelled Stan, who was intent on heading back to his room for some shuteye.

With that, the guy took out a baseball bat and chased Nance around the hotel, with the others scrambling to stop both of them. It turned out to be no harm, no foul, and order was restored.

When the guys got back from Italy, I was happy to see them again. I was keeping busy with school and baseball, but they were my brothers now, and I enjoyed hanging out with them.

As graduation approached, I received a request from a Little League group in Highland Park to speak at their awards dinner. My initial thought was that they couldn't get anyone else on the team to come to the banquet, so they settled on me. But it made some sense once I realized they wanted me because of my baseball connection. My plan was to talk about playing two sports in college and how challenging it could be at times, especially with classes.

When I arrived there with Bob Merker, one of my roommates, I was pleasantly surprised. Between 150 and 200 people were there, and nearly every one of them seemed to know details about Rutgers basketball. They knew the opponents we had beaten, the scores, and the memorable plays that had occurred. They even had a sign that said, "Welcome Mr. 100," and several people came up to me and said, "We love you guys. You made us proud."

All of it made me realize, two months after we played our last game, that the Rutgers basketball team had made an indelible impression not only on our fellow students and adults around the state, but also on young people. It made me feel very good and I told the guys when I spoke to each one.

I graduated from Rutgers in May of 1976. It was a beautiful, sunny day, and we were all pretty happy and proud. Scherer and I were the latest in a long line of Rutgers basketball players, including Steve Duthie, Steve DiPeri, and Jim Valvano, who had lived in Century Apartments, apartment 2C, over the past fifteen years. We stayed there until the end of May, but that was largely because it took that long to clean the apartment so we wouldn't have to forfeit our deposit.

I was very gratified during the graduation ceremony with the reception our basketball seniors received. When they called up the graduating players to receive their diplomas, there was a loud, enthusiastic cheer from those in attendance. I was reminded again that we had made a lasting impression on the university and the state, and that despite the ending, we had given the people of Rutgers and New Jersey a memory to cherish and a season everyone could be proud of.

Our team was a unique group of individuals, not just from a personality standpoint, but from a playing-style standpoint. And Coach Young knew it.

"I'd love to play their type of basketball every year, but it's hard to find the kind of quickness they had," Young said. "That group was not only good, but exciting. They were mentally tough, with a real killer instinct. And they loved to play. I never had to worry about those guys. They thoroughly enjoyed the game."

Phil Sellers had the final word, which was only fitting:

"We really had a lot of fun that season," said Sellers. "We were a together team. White guys, Black guys, it didn't make a difference. We played together and hung out together. We created some excitement, and we accomplished more than any Rutgers team ever has."

THREADS OF NOSTALGIA: FANS' MEMORIES FROM THE 1975–76 SEASON

OVER THE COURSE OF WRITING this book, I spoke to every living player and coach of the 1975–76 Rutgers basketball team, and one theme consistently came to the forefront. Each of them made a point of acknowledging the incredible support we received from our fans and how essential they were to our success.

As a result, they became an integral part of the story I wanted to tell. I decided quite early in the process that there would be a chapter about some of the people whose dedication and support might otherwise have been overlooked.

I wanted people outside of the program to share their stories and memories. But fifty years later, where to begin? First, I contacted Al Reicheg, the president of the Court Club, who not only explained the makeup of his group but also volunteered to write a letter about the book and post it on the club's website.

In his letter, Al asked people who were fans from that era to send their memories directly to me. The response was enthusiastic and heartening, and what was interesting was how vivid those memories were. I had assumed that only people who were directly related to the team (players, coaches, etc.) would remember that time with such detail. I was wrong.

So this chapter serves as a thank you to the best fans any team could want to accompany them along the ride of our lives. These are their words.

ELIZABETH (BETSY) SHOTT

Douglass College, Class of 1977

Along with my friends, I went to every game at the Barn and Madison Square Garden. It remains the best sports experience I ever enjoyed. I remember the entire team, you included. Freshmen James Bailey and Abdel Anderson were the final pieces. They fit perfectly with starters Phil Sellers, Mike Dabney, Eddie Jordan, and Hollis Copeland. And you had the perfect coach. I will never forget Coach Tom Young's white towel.

Coach Young's running style was perfect for you guys. It wore down your opponents. No three-point shot but the scores were always so high. I remember standing in line with our IDs for tickets and then squeezing into the balcony at the Barn and getting loud enough for the paint chips to fall. I remember one of the cheer squad members carrying a pole with school pennants of the teams you had beaten.

And I remember those NCAA games. I did not go to Philly. I think it was during spring break. I was headed to Florida. I still can't believe I did that. Philly was so close. Mostly I remember that final regular season game at the Barn. The nail biter against St. Bonaventure. The perfect regular season was complete and then the team went on that bus and rode around campus to ring the bell at Old Queens. What a night! I recently turned seventy and my years at RU were wonderful and the ride you took us on was tremendous. Thanks!!!

ROBERT MERKER

Rutgers College, Class of 1976

I know it has been fifty years, but so much happened during that basketball season that sticks out for me. I came to Rutgers from nearby

Metuchen as an eighteen-year-old student and tennis player. My parents were glad I chose Rutgers because it enabled them to watch my tennis matches. I also was glad I chose the school because it had a great academic reputation and it allowed me to play in a Division I program.

During my freshman year I met Jeff Kleinbaum and Bruce Scherer in my psychology class and, as they say, "the rest is history." Once I started hanging out with them, along with Brian Perkins, my path changed drastically. I can think of so many things that happened as a result of the players becoming celebrities on campus. I was the door watcher at home games, which was great fun but also stressful at times because the crowds were huge and people were offering me a lot of money to let them in. They offered just about anything, but I held my ground.

Once in the gym, I sat under the basket, and it was an incredible experience. The team would run out to the Rutgers fight song being performed by the Rutgers Pep Band and the sound was deafening. The floor reverberated even though it was just warm-ups. I have gone to professional and college sporting events most of my life but I had never seen, heard, or felt anything like the Rutgers crowd. The paint chips and smell of chlorine from behind the wall added so much more to it as well.

After games, we usually went to Olde Queens Tavern, and then, late at night, we went home. Usually, when I got to our apartment, there were a handful of girls waiting for you and Bruce just to get a glimpse and maybe get invited in. You were always gentlemen to them, and you politely talked with them even though you were quite tired.

I see people all the time who remember the Final Four season and they all say the same thing. It was the best time of their lives. This book should put the icing on the cake for many people. I can't wait to read it.

CHRIS JENNINGS

Rutgers College, Class of 1978

We had just witnessed perfection. In the jam-packed Barn, the Rutgers basketball team had just staged a furious comeback against a St.

Bonaventure team that had played a near perfect game. The twenty-sixth win tied a ribbon on an undefeated regular season. Upon exiting this beloved relic of a gymnasium, even the cool rain that was falling could not dampen the spirits of the delirious crowd now spilling onto College Avenue.

It had been announced that this unprecedented Rutgers achievement would be commemorated at Old Queens. I am the fourth of what is five generations of Rutgers graduates. My grandfather, Kenneth (RC Class of 1924), was a professor of journalism here for thirty-eight years. I was well steeped in Rutgers tradition. My girlfriend, her roommate, and I had not missed a home game all season. We all headed to Old Queens, the original building of the pre-revolutionary college where tradition dictates that the bell in its tower should be rung for exceptional accomplishments by members of the university.

Suddenly my girlfriend and her roommate veered off course. It was difficult to locate them among the throng of revelers. After I caught up to them, I asked, "where are you two going?" They replied, "We're going to Olde Queens." They were heading to Olde Queens Tavern, the wildly popular watering hole for students. The scene at Olde Queens Tavern was surreal, almost akin in my mind to the crowds at Times Square on New Year's Eve. By this time, the entire New Brunswick community was here to party. As the bells in the tower rang out through the night sky, I was aware that I was a witness to a celebration that I would most likely never see again. Perfection is rarely attained.

DR. ALAN VENOOK

Co–Sports Editor of The Daily Targum, *the student newspaper, during the 1975–76 season*

I attended thirty of the thirty-three games that season and had witnessed and written about one of just twenty (as of today) undefeated regular seasons in college basketball history and also sat courtside as Bob Knight's Indiana team completed its undefeated championship season. And yet, the memory that sprung to mind was a story I wrote for the

Mugrat edition (the annual spoof issue) of the *Targum* in January of that year.

The headline—"Sellers faces NCAA charges; Forfeitures likely"—went viral (in 1976 terms) when the Associated Press did not initially check the source and put it out on the wire (it really was a wire) before deleting it forever. (An FYI: I cleared the story with both Tom Young and Phil Sellers to warn them but also to make sure it was not true. Sellers found it hilarious, Young did not.)

And the highlights, the memorable plays, snatching victory from the jaws of defeat? My memory failed me. Other than the Eddie Jordan airball against Manhattan and the Pete Molloy bricked free throw in the NCAA tournament I could recall no particular in-game moments in vivid detail. No posturizing dunks? (Dunking was not allowed.) No game winning buzzer-beating threes? (There was no three-point line in 1976.) Hoping to jog my memory, I turned to the Rutgers Library Archives and revisited the season through *The Daily Targum*. And then I was again reminded of what a special season it really was.

Only ten of Rutgers's games were at the Barn, which means it won twenty-one road or neutral site games before getting to Philadelphia. In a span of twenty-six games over three months, Rutgers won all but three of those games by double digits. In an era with neither a shot clock nor a three-point line, Rutgers *AVERAGED* 93.3 points per game and its margin of victory was 16.4 points per game. What was memorable was how much better Rutgers was than every team it played, until it was not.

ANNMARIE GORDA

Super fan / She was sixteen when we played in the Final Four

You have no idea how excited I am to celebrate the fiftieth anniversary of the best team, in my opinion, that the Rutgers basketball program has ever seen. I went up into my attic to ensure I could locate my memorabilia. I have a scrapbook of newspaper articles, a Madison Square Garden program, ticket stubs and individual programs offered at the

Barn for some of the games, and many other great souvenirs. I have vivid memories of my trips to Madison Square Garden on the train. We made a poster saying "Rutgers #1" and walked through each train car with the sign. It was well received! People clapped and cheered when they saw it.

That season was electric. The mood was something I had never experienced before. I reached out to Coach Tom Young asking if I could attend a practice or wait after a game for the team to sign my scrapbook. I received a letter back telling me I could purchase a yearbook through the athletic department. I was crushed. I was about sixteen at the time. Being sixteen, I also had a huge crush on Mark Conlin. I knew he was married with a child, but I was sixteen! Lol. I even have a photo of him at his graduation. One of my brothers graduated the same year as him.

The atmosphere in the Barn was amazing. The volume was so loud. The team was exciting to watch and everyone could feel it. It was palpable. It was a riveting time in Rutgers basketball history, and I am so grateful to have been a part of it. If there is ever a reunion or celebration when the whole team gathers, I would still love to get my scrapbook signed by the team. I am fortunate to have Phil Sellers autograph on a program.

Over the years, I often thought about that great season and team members. Such fond memories!

CLIFF SMITH

Rutgers College, 1979
Loyal Son, 2004

I was a freshman when Jeff and his teammates made a remarkable run to an undefeated regular season and our only Final Four appearance. Has it really been almost fifty years? When reflecting on those times, I go back to my first game. We were already 5–0 and hosting UConn, who I recall had a pretty good player in Tony Hanson. I remember having to get in line early and waiting in the cold for the Barn doors to open. Little did I know how that one game, that one experience, would affect my entire life. I remember the chants of "Who's he?" when each UConn starter was announced—even Hanson.

By the way, when we played Navy later in the year, I still laugh how that chant changed to "Who's he, Sir?" I thought that was great.

Now, to be fair, as much as Phil Sellers looked like a man among boys out there, the person who equally caught my eye was Eddie Jordan. I thought he was terrific. Sellers was the heart and soul of that team. There's no question about that. But I thought Jordan was the one who made it all happen. He seemed to get everyone involved with his pinpoint passing. His defense was also outstanding. And that brings to mind that suffocating full-court press, which became the team's trade-mark. It just seemed like Jordan was in the middle of everything. I also remember later telling my boys that Jordan did all that dribbling and his hand was really on top of the ball.

DARRYL GURNEY

Rutgers College, Class of 1978

Our long devotion to RU hoops started during the 1975–76 undefeated regular season. We went to as many games as we could, with school-work always present, and at a time when one had to wait in a line outside overnight in order to secure admission to the games. A bunch of us had a Poli-Sci 101 midterm the following morning first period the day of the St. Bonaventure game (thanks a lot Dr. Benjamin Barber, our professor), so we crowded around a little black-and-white TV with the NJ TV station and its sketchy reception and watched the win that cemented the 26–0 regular season and came up with our "Undefeated" gyration of a dance.

I saw Phil Sellers dominate Beaver Smith and St. John's at Madison Square Garden in the ECAC finals (after seeing "The Thrill" score his two thousandth point in Rose Hill Gym at Fordham earlier in the season) and I was there to witness the Pete Molloy free-throw miss in Providence as we held on to beat Princeton 54–53. On Thursday, March 18, of that season, we headed to Greensboro but due to our late start (someone in our group had an early midterm) we stopped at University of Delaware during the first game of the East Regionals. After RU beat UConn for the second time that season we continued on our overnight drive to Greensboro, NC, in order to make the Elite 8 matchup of Rutgers vs. VMI. We had a great Friday touring the area and came up with our four tickets in the upper deck for the Saturday afternoon game.

Following that, we drove back Sunday, at the time spring break was starting, and crashed in my apartment Sunday night, but home for my friends was still in Brett Hall (open for select students) so we ended up there on the fourth floor, where our friend and preceptor and, coincidentally, student council president Stever Holtzman greeted us. He told us that students had already started to line up outside the Student Center in the cold in order to hopefully end up with one of the 250 student tickets allocated for the Final Four (they were being distributed on that Wednesday) and on his urging the Rutgers administration had decided to open up the Student Center for those to wait.

He presented us with a proposition: Would we be willing to be student "marshals" and monitor those who would be waiting in line? Our "pay"? We would have the opportunity of being the first to purchase our Final Four tickets ($27.50 apiece for the entire Final Four).

I have vivid memories of the Final Four experience! Unfortunately, once we arrived with our front-row seats (saved ticket stub says row 2, seat 2 for some reason) I forever jinxed the program by saying "I can get used to this!"

We were seated by the players' path to the court (Kent Benson of Indiana actually pushed me out of the way as he led his team out) and were right there during that tough loss to Michigan (to this day I think we could have/should have beaten them) and then for the game against UCLA (they were dominant, geez what a talented team; Marques Johnson was a man among boys) and thus started our Rutgers basketball addiction.

Thanks for giving us memories we will never forget.

MIKE BRILL

Rutgers College, Class of 1977

I was the President of the Rutgers College Class of 1977. I remember Jeff and some of his teammates not only from basketball but as acquaintances at Century Apartments. I was close friends with Larry Martz and Mark Zimmerman, who were Jeff's neighbors there. Anyway, I was a trumpet player in the pep band, so we followed the team during this incredible journey/achievement. As you may recall, the Barn was tiny, so the pep band members had to share playing time at the basketball games on a rotation system.

On the team's trip down to Greensboro, NC, I did not make the list to play my trumpet for that series of games, so I drove there to watch as a spectator. One of my friends, who I will call JT from *Targum*, needed a ride to the games, so she hitched one with me. We arrived at a no-frills Days Inn in Greensboro in the early morning hours the day before the game. I went right to sleep, as did another friend, but JT decided to take a huge, white bedsheet and a can of red spray paint and headed to the pool. She spread the bed sheet on the cement by the pool and painted "Phil-Adel-Phia Freedom" on the sheet.

To our surprise, we heard her banging on the sliding glass door of our room at four a.m., where she told us we had to get the hell out of this hotel. The spray paint seeped through the sheet and onto the cement around the pool.

So at four a.m. we left the hotel and slept the rest of the time in the car outside the Greensboro Coliseum. Who cares…WE WON!

JOHN WOODING

Former Photography Editor, The Daily Targum

Rutgers basketball enjoyed the greatest season in its history in 1975–76, and I was lucky enough to have a front-row seat throughout! For a young Rutgers fan from New Brunswick, the advent of the Phil

Sellers–Mike Dabney era was a memorable one. After originally attending Syracuse as a freshman, I transferred to Rutgers in the fall of 1975 and was trying to make inroads on campus. One of my first stops was at the *Targum*, the award-winning student daily newspaper. With a dream of becoming a photojournalist, I started as a member of the photography staff and began writing for the sports department.

What a wonderful time for that! The football team was on the upswing, and the basketball team had just broken through on the national stage with its first-ever NCAA tournament appearance in 1975. It was a magical sophomore year for me. The football team overcame some early season missteps to win its final seven games and finish 9–2 (and then went 11–0 the next season). The basketball team's memorable 1975–76 season has been well-documented and celebrated, and rightfully so. The Barn rocked the entire season, and Rutgers's home away from home—Madison Square Garden—was always exciting. I had a front-row seat for so many great wins—literally, because I would sit on the baseline as a photographer for the *Targum*.

Early season wins over Purdue at Madison Square Garden, and Seton Hall at home, served notice that Rutgers would be a team to be reckoned with. As the season marched into the homestretch, Rutgers knocked off No. 15, Princeton, 75–62 on the road. The overtime win over Manhattan two weeks later came with so much intrigue, as point guard extraordinaire Eddie Jordan sat out most of the first forty minutes before leading Rutgers to victory in the overtime ("Why did Jordan sit out until overtime?" was the prevailing question throughout campus). It was the "ECAC Game of the Week" with Marv Albert and Bucky Waters calling the action on NBC-TV!

The season was topped off by the madhouse win in the regular season finale against St. Bonaventure, and the two great victories, again at the Garden, over LIU and St. John's in the ECAC Metro championship. Of course, the NCAA run to the Final Four assured that the memory of that year would always be there. The summer after the Final Four, I ran into Tom Young's great assistant coach and right-hand man Joe Boylan, in the Barn. We had a brief conversation before he kiddingly asked, "What school are you going to transfer to next—

Louisville?" After all, Syracuse in my freshman year went to the Final Four and then Rutgers duplicated that feat the following year. Two years of college and two Final Fours—amazing! No more transfers for me, though, as I knew I was at home, at Rutgers, where I was meant to be!

RICHARD FEDER

Class of 1975

I was an avid basketball fan all through my four years at Rutgers and have many fine memories of sitting packed in on the bleachers in the close confines of the Barn cheering for my Scarlet Knights. Loud and boisterous, the Barn's uniqueness certainly gave Rutgers a home court advantage. With the high humid conditions because of the adjacent Rutgers swimming pool together with the din from the noise reverberating off the huge side wall separating pool and basketball court, our goal as loyal fans was to create such a crescendo that paint would peel from the ceiling. Certainly, a unique venue in which to play basketball.

Although no one could expect an undefeated season in 1975, the 1974-75 team was high performing, led by stars Phil Sellars and Mike Dabney and freshman Hollis Copeland. I remember that team started the season in Hawaii and color photos of the team enjoying palm trees and beaches made their way back to wintery New Brunswick. The team's success in 1974 led to an invitation to play in the NCAA Tournament, although they lost in the first round. Yet, with nearly the entire team returning and the addition of some key incoming freshman (James Bailey and Abdel Anderson), the 1975-76 Rutgers team gave us fans great hope that something special was in the offing.

However, before the undefeated season began, a number of significant life events occurred. First, I graduated from Rutgers University in May of 1975. Shortly thereafter, I began my work career as an insurance adjuster. And on February 7, 1976 in snowy and cold New Brunswick at Kirkpatrick Chapel on Rutgers University campus, I married my Douglas College sweetheart, Lynda Kennedy. This was followed by our wedding reception at the Elks Club in New Brunswick and our first night as a married couple in a hotel in New Brunswick.

But…*wait*…after beating West Virginia in Madison Square Garden on February 5, 1976 to go 17 and 0, Rutgers was next scheduled to play Navy on Saturday night, February 7, at the Barn. Yes, the night of my wedding day. What a dilemma! A lifelong Rutgers fan. An undefeated season on the line. But come on, my wedding night? Well, *no*, I did not leave my marital bed to travel to the Barn. However, and this may indicate why we will be married 50 years in February 2026, my new bride allowed me to put the game on the television in the room where *I* saw Rutgers handle the Midshipmen, winning by 15 points. I must say all and all, it was a very good night.

The last regular season game of the undefeated 75-76 team was against St. Bonaventure at the Barn. For years, as an avid sports fan, I had seen the likes of Notre Dame, Michigan, and USC get favorable calls by officials game after game. Top rankings and highly successful seasons were somehow achieved by these teams time after time from what I saw as bogus calls by officials. It is supposed to go 50/50, but not with these teams. With minutes left in the final game, the Bonnies led by seven points and Rutger's undefeated season was about to become a pipe dream. I remember watching on TV as the Fates decided to bleed Scarlet. One call after another suddenly went our way and the team rallied to win by 5 points, guaranteeing an undefeated regular season.

The Final Four game against Michigan was a disappointment. Again, watching in my living room in my River Edge, NJ apartment, I still have memories of Ricky Green blazing by everyone up and down the court, leading Michigan to victory. I remember so many shots by our boys just missing, so many that had fallen all season. It just was not meant to be. Looking back 50 years later, the joys of watching Rutgers basketball that season still resonates. How proud I am over the accomplishments of that team. What joy and excitement it brought to all Rutgers fans.

SKIP ROACH

Rutgers Class of 1978

1976 gave us Apple and Microsoft. These companies would go on to forever change the course of humanity. On a lighter note, Van Morrison and Bruce shook the Barn. 1976 gave us Nurse Ratched, the space shuttle, *The Gong Show*, and *Roots* by Alex Haley. Politically, we had Patty Hearst, Jimmy Carter, Gerald Ford, and we unfairly condemned those who served and then came home from war.

In the world of sports, 1976 was an exciting year too. The thing that stands out to me and to most of the people I associated with took place in New Brunswick, New Jersey: the Rutgers basketball team compiled a record of 28-0 during the regular season!

The excitement was incredible as each game brought out the best in our players and fans, fighting for one of the 2800 hottest seats in town, cramming the Barn. Nobody wanted to play us and nobody really wanted to play us at home. We averaged over 93 points per game without having a 3-point line or being allowed to dunk. Give Sellers the ball and get out of the way.

It was a great time. The players bonded and the entire Rutgers community was behind them. The coach, Tom Young, was a task master, never posting a losing season as head coach, and it was clear that something special was at hand. We would have to wait until 2006 and Louisville to feel that same level again (Rutgers Football Team).

MOSS KLEIN

Rutgers graduate and longtime sportswriter for The Star-Ledger *of Newark, NJ. He covered Rutgers basketball for the 1975–76 season before switching to the New York Yankees beat.*

For nearly the final two months of Rutgers's remarkable 1975–76 season, each game carried special significance for me: If Rutgers won, the perfect season and the hottest sports story in New Jersey would continue and I would keep doing the job I loved.

If Rutgers lost, it would signal a career change for me, a jarring shift of assignments. And until the end, as far as it could go, Rutgers kept winning.

But from game to game, there was always the uncertainty to deal with, and the suitcase that would accompany me out of that treasured comfort zone stayed packed.

This was the situation: A month or so before the start of spring training, in early January, *The Star-Ledger*'s longtime Yankees beat writer, Jim Ogle, announced he was retiring. I was next in line for that coveted beat. But I was the Rutgers beat writer, and it was decided by the editors that Rutgers at that point, still undefeated, was a more important story than Yankees spring training—especially when Ogle, who lived near the Yankees' spring training camp in Fort Lauderdale, was willing to continue covering until I got there.

So on it went…covering through the regular season and beyond. If Rutgers lost, I would get on a plane the next day for Fort Lauderdale to start my new assignment in that new—and somewhat scary—world. It would mean leaving behind a great assignment and a bunch of writers who had become close friends, and a coaching staff and other Rutgers people who had become friends, and postgame gatherings at Olde Queens and Corner Tavern, the popular bars where everybody knew your name.

I was a Rutgers graduate, class of 1972, and still lived in an old house on the crosstown Douglass campus. Rutgers, of course, kept winning. all the way to the Final Four, and my Fort Lauderdale suitcase stayed packed. Then came the loss to Michigan in Philadelphia and I stayed for the Monday consolation game, a loss to UCLA, then made the drive home to New Brunswick, with a quick check of the suitcase and a flight to Fort Lauderdale the next day for the start of my new world. I had some catching up to do with the Yankees, with only a week left in spring training, but the wait was well worth it.

BRIAN PERKINS

Brian Perkins is not only a longtime fan of Rutgers basketball; he was my roommate all four years at school. He was actively being recruited by Rutgers for basketball but wound up being "first man out" of our recruiting class when Phil Sellers and Mike Dabney committed to Rutgers late in the recruiting season. Brian still chose to attend Rutgers and played jayvee ball with us when that was still a thing. He has been chairman of the Rutgers Board of Overseers and a member of the Board of Trustees.

My first and enduring memory of the 1975–76 team is from September of 1972 just before the school year started. Several of the highly re-cruited players were walking onto the court in the Barn where they were about to play their first pickup game together with some return-ing players…and me. Phil Sellers appeared on the court with his now trademark scowl. A man among boys. Mike Dabney (Dip) was a gazelle on the court and could jump out of the gym. Jeff Kleinbaum, my roommate for four years, was built like a tank that went a hundred miles per hour, but on chicken legs!

Bruce Scherer (a roommate for three years) and Mike Palko were doing alley-oop dunks before it was a thing (no dunking was allowed back then in games). I thought I was a pretty good high school player, but if I harbored any resentment about not being an official part of the incoming recruiting class, that thought evaporated about five minutes into the game. These guys were special.

Flash forward four years to the last game of the regular season when it looked very much like we were going to lose to St. Bonaventure at the Barn and end the magical run. I was sitting in the first row under the basket in front of the Rutgers bench. It was late in the game, and we desperately needed a defensive stop. A St. Bonaventure player missed a shot, and I distinctly remember two hands rising above all other play-ers to grab the rebound, which helped preserve the win. It was Phil Sellers. With a scowl on his face. He just wanted it more.

Flash forward one more time, this time forty-seven years later. I was relating this memory to Phil while visiting him in the hospital a day before his untimely death in September of 2023. He remembered the play instantly. When I asked him what he most remembered about that special team, he started to cry when he told me that it was all about the special guys he played with…Dip, Jeff, Bruce, Mike, Eddie Jordan, Hollis Copeland, Mark Conlin, Steve Hefele, James Bailey, Abdel Anderson, Stan Nance…all of whom Phil told me either called or visited to comfort him in his last days. What a team.

ECHOES OF YESTERDAY: MY FINAL THOUGHTS

WHEN I RETIRED FROM TEACHING and coaching, I, like many new retirees, worried about how I would fill my time. I had just spent forty years of my life working in a profession I loved, and I always assumed that I would work indefinitely. As time went by, I knew I wanted to spend more time with my wife and travel more. Deborah and I made plans for our family and began mapping out our travel adventures for the upcoming year. Then, in June of 2024, I met a passionate Rutgers fan who was well-versed in the accomplishments of our Final Four team. When I mentioned that I had played for that team, he immediately recognized my name and we spent quite a while reminiscing. This kind of encounter has happened frequently over the years.

Toward the end of our conversation, he mentioned that he had seen a documentary about our 1975–76 team on the Big Ten Network and lamented that he had never read a book dedicated solely to our team. "Curious," he asked, "do you know where I can get one?"

It struck me that there were many books about basketball that mentioned our team, but none had been written specifically about us. For months, the idea of this missing narrative lingered in my mind.

With the fiftieth anniversary of our Final Four year approaching, I felt compelled to create a definitive account of our glorious year, one that could also transport fans into the inner workings of our journey. Reflecting on the passage of time, I realized that we had already lost

Phil Sellers and two of our coaches, Head Coach Tom Young and Assistant Coach Joe Boylan. Over the next few decades, we will lose others too. This realization convinced me to write this book.

In December of 2024, I met with my college roommates, Bruce Scherer, Brian Perkins, and Bob Merker, for lunch at Rafferty's, a restaurant in New Brunswick, NJ, and shared my plans. They were very supportive but also curious about how I would proceed. We discussed it during lunch, and we all agreed that it was a good idea to move forward.

I then reached out to each player on the team, and to a man, they expressed their full support. Stan Nance said it was about time someone took on this project. Hollis Copeland assured me he would assist in any way he could. Eddie Jordan's response nearly brought me to tears: "Jeff, this book will be our legacy. Someday we will all be gone, and who will remember that 'once there was a time'? You need to do this—not just for us, but for everyone who considers this a significant part of their lifestyle."

When I spoke to Mike Dabney, he pointed out that no other team in Rutgers history had impacted so many lives. Conversations with Dick Lloyd and Dick Vitale were equally encouraging. Their perspectives carried weight, as they had recruited me and many of the pivotal players from the 1975–76 team. Their enthusiasm reinforced my belief that writing about our experiences could bring cherished memories to the forefront. When Vitale remarked that he believed the book would be a "prime timer," I decided for sure to do it!

The interviews we conducted took me back beyond the 1975–76 season to my senior year in high school, when I first met Dick Vitale. He was a supportive presence throughout the writing process, embodying the same warmth and charisma viewers see on television. His generosity with his time helped breathe life into the beginning of this remarkable story.

Conversing with Dick Lloyd, my first head coach at Rutgers, was a profound experience. I owe him tremendous gratitude, not only for bringing me to Rutgers, but also for treating me with unwavering respect and teaching me aspects of the game I needed to learn. He recounted how Rutgers made the groundbreaking decision to offer scholarships for the first time, starting with my freshman year in 1972–73, and how we almost lost Phil Sellers during that process because he had awarded the last allotted scholarship to me.

I am eternally grateful that my recruitment ended up not preventing Phil from becoming the greatest player in program history, since Coach Lloyd and the athletic department needed to find the money for an additional scholarship to get him into the fold after he changed his college choice from Notre Dame to Rutgers.

As a head coach myself at New Jersey high schools (Spotswood, Union, Middletown North, Whippany Park), I understand that head coaches often receive little credit when teams are winning, but they bear much of the blame when things go awry. Assistant coaches, despite their critical roles, often go unrecognized, especially when a team wins thirty-one of thirty-three games in a season, as we did. We were fortunate to have three outstanding assistant coaches whose contributions were vital to our success.

Joe Boylan was one of the kindest people I have ever worked with. He had a quiet strength, and when he spoke, wisdom flowed from him. He was beloved by every player. His relationship with Tom Young was remarkable; they complemented each other perfectly, with Joe's calm demeanor balancing Tom's more animated personality and quirks. On some of our long road trips, they would bring their families, and watching them interact as parents and husbands brought out a heartwarming side of their personalities that people outside the team never had the chance to experience.

Assistant Coach John McFadden, who played at Rutgers before joining Dick Lloyd's staff in 1971 and then Tom Young's in 1972, is one of the brightest basketball minds I know. Even today, he continues to coach players and stays up-to-date on modern strategies. His insights are intelligent and enlightening.

Currently an assistant coach at Cherokee High School in South Jersey, Coach McFadden has helped Head Coach Ron Powell's teams achieve an incredible 237–42 record over the past ten years, including a state championship in 2020.

Art Perry, the last assistant coach to join our staff, is a genuine and selfless man. He came to Rutgers from American University, where he played for and then coached alongside Tom Young. Art has remained connected with us, always checking in to ensure we are doing well. We are fortunate to have had him as our coach.

Our team managers were dedicated and skilled individuals who became integral to our journey. Pete Horowitz, a loyal Rutgers sports fan, has held season basketball tickets since 1988. He loves discussing Rutgers basketball and has a remarkable memory of our undefeated season. His fellow managers, Scott Walton and Ken Eisler, formed a close bond with each other that was akin to the brotherhood we shared as players.

Throughout this process, I have reconnected with many individuals from my time at Rutgers who have offered invaluable support. Kathleen Conlin, Mark's wife and our team's "house mother," tops the list. She has played a vital role in keeping us connected over the years. She has also been our point of contact for various matters and has generously provided access to memorabilia and contact information for those I needed to reach.

I have also encountered numerous people who have enriched my life since my arrival at Rutgers. One of the most impactful was Abe Suydam, who recently passed away. Abe was devoted to Rutgers basketball and played a significant role in easing the transition of players from high school to college. He and his wife, Ann, often hosted us at their farm, where we shared countless hours discussing Rutgers basketball by their fireplace.

One summer, when some of us stayed at Rutgers to hone our skills at the Barn, Abe hired us to work on his farm. While I loved Abe, working in a hayloft in the sweltering summer heat was not my idea of fun or love. Nevertheless, our bond with Abe and Ann grew immensely, and their children, Robyn, Sally, and Ryke, have also played crucial roles in this journey. Ryke, in particular, has been a tremendous asset for this book.

As I sought out memories for this project, I connected with individuals I had not known before, all of whom shared similar experiences during our time at Rutgers in the 1970s. Steve Shapiro, a lifelong Rutgers sports fan, introduced me to a group of fraternity brothers who have maintained their bond for fifty years. Their dedication to discussing and analyzing Rutgers sports is both impressive and inspiring. I had the pleasure of participating in one of their Zoom meetings, which turned into a lively two-and-a-half-hour question-and-answer session. I've since met with them for lunch and look forward to continuing our discussions.

Their contributions, including articles and box scores from the 1975–76 season, have been invaluable. Thank you, Stanley Stempler, Stuart Reiser, Bill Kurtzer, Michael Nord, Clinton Plietz, Jonathan Mann, and Steve Shapiro, for your continued support of Rutgers basketball and your undying love for our Final Four team.

I would be remiss if I did not acknowledge Annmarie Gorda and her husband, Keith, and their son, Keith Jr. Annmarie's memories of our team, which are included in this book, touched me deeply. An ardent supporter of the Final Four team, she has followed our careers over the years and generously offered her collection of memorabilia, including a complete scrapbook with newspaper articles from that season. I am committed to honoring her and the others who have generously written stories about their time watching our team play.

Very early in the process, I realized that I was not strong enough on the computer as I needed to be to write a book without it taking years to complete. To that end, I enlisted two family members, my daughter Michelle and my niece, Isabella, to teach me the intricacies I needed to know. Thank you to both of you for answering my frantic calls at all hours of the day and night when things got lost, or when I needed to insert items quickly. I love you both.

My wife, Deborah, was extremely supportive, as I knew she would be, when I broached the idea of writing this book. She told me that I owed it to myself to do this, and she has helped me immeasurably each and every day. She was my rock all the way through the project.

My daughters, Laura and Michelle, and my new son-in-law, Laura's husband Mike, were so happy to see me work on this project too. They obviously were not around during the Final Four year, but they had heard so many stories, because people liked to talk to me about it in their company. I sensed that they were proud of me for doing this, and that was great, considering how proud I am of them for all they have accomplished.

A very special "thank you" also goes to my college roommate and close friend, Brian Perkins, whose memories are included in this book as well. Brian told me at the beginning of the project that he would help me in any way he could. That absolutely was an understatement. Brian has been by my side from the beginning to the end. He used his incredible skills as a marketing expert to develop the plan we used to promote and market the book. We spoke every day, and he became as engulfed in the project as I have been. We were brothers in every sense of the word for over fifty years, but these last several months have brought our relationship to another level.

Finally, I want to pay tribute to my teammates. I can't write in this space how I feel about each one of them, so I will only say that since I started working on this project, each one of them stepped up to help me in incredible ways, just as I expected. They are engrained in my heart, and I couldn't ask for a better family of brothers.

Five decades have passed since the seniors on our Final Four team took off our sneakers for the last time as college players. We have reunited numerous times, solidifying our bond as a unique team in Rutgers history. My wife affectionately refers to us as the "team that never dies."

We have celebrated our anniversaries at home basketball games, including our tenth, fifteenth, twentieth, twenty-fifth, thirtieth, and fortieth (our forty-fifth anniversary celebration was canceled because of the COVID pandemic), and we have been inducted as a team into the Rutgers Athletic Hall of Fame.

We even reenacted our official 1975–76 team photo during Eddie Jordan's introduction as Rutgers's head coach. I remain hopeful that we are on the brink of establishing ourselves as a consistent contender in the NCAA tournament for years to come. Throughout the ups and downs of Rutgers basketball over the past fifty years, one constant has remained: the unwavering support of the fans. The energy and excitement at every Rutgers home game are palpable, setting a standard that will always endure.

For the past six months, I have been transported back to that time, reliving the moments that defined our college years. I can visualize the shots that found their mark and those that fortunately fell short, like Pete Molloy's free-throw miss that landed in Mike Dabney's hands as we escaped Princeton in the first round of the NCAA tournament.

I remember the defensive prowess of Mike Palko, Hollis Copeland's incredible athleticism, Steve Hefele's jump shots, Mark Conlin's tenacity and ball handling, James Bailey's rejections (to the third row), Abdel Anderson's signature shooting style, Eddie Jordan's floor leadership and ability to run the fast break, Bruce Scherer's smooth-as-silk jumpers, and Stan Nance's relentless hustle and desire. The fluid, seemingly effortless athleticism of Mike Dabney and the greatness of Phil Sellers will endure as long as Rutgers plays basketball.

I see our dedicated assistant coaches, who were instrumental in our development, and I will never forget Tom Young, our coach, mentor, and friend, pacing the sidelines, towel in hand or clenched in his mouth, leading us through our incredible run.

Our lives are forever intertwined through our shared history and love for each other and Rutgers basketball. If that legacy endures, I am more than content; I am thrilled and honored. Let us cherish every moment we have together, both in person and in spirit. And most of all…Let's go, Rutgers!

SECTION 3: CELEBRATIONS

Tom Young accepts congratulations from Princeton's coach Pete Carrill after critical win at Jadwin Gym

Tom Young is surrounded by the crowd after beating St. Bonaventure to go undefeated

President Bloustein of Rutgers looks over the crowd, estimated at 10,000, after the team beat St. Bonaventure to secure an undefeated regular season

Nancy Young (Tom's wife) shows
her pride in her husband's team

Phil "The Thrill" Sellers and a young fan
kneel at center court of the Barn after
Sellers passed Bob Lloyd to become
Rutgers All-time leading scorer.

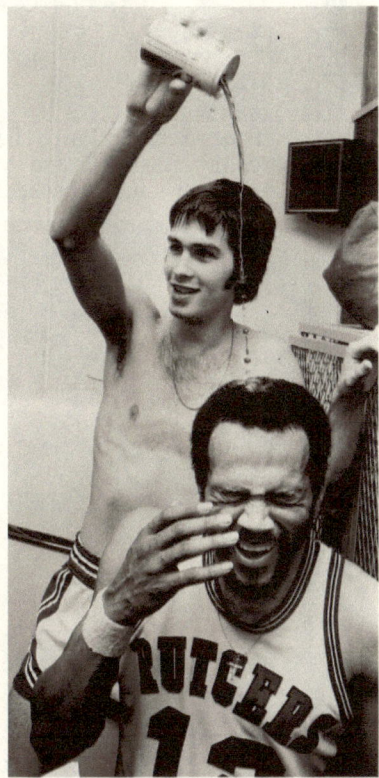

Mark Conlin pours champagne
over the head of Phil Sellers
after the team beat VMI to
advance to the Final Four

A Look into the Future

Bruce Scherer, Phil Sellers, President Bloustein, Robert
Smith, Asst. AD, and Mike Dabney admire a model of
Rutger's future basketball home (completed in 1978)

Tom Young and Team gather at center court
of Madison Square Garden after defeating
St. Johns for the ECAC Championship

FINAL FOUR TEAM

THE 1975-76 RUTGERS UNIVERSITY BASKETBALL TEAM (31-2)
ECAC METROPOLITAN CHAMPION
NCAA EAST REGIONAL CHAMPION
NCAA FINAL FOUR

WHATEVER HAPPENED TO...?

T HE FRIENDSHIPS FORGED DURING THE 1975–76 Final Four team remain as strong as ever for the twelve Rutgers players who were part of that memorable journey. A half-century later, we are still a close-knit group, with the bond among us evident during the many reunions Rutgers has held to honor the team.

So, what happened to everyone on that 1975–76 team after college? What follows is a recap of our lives and careers.

COACHING STAFF

Tom Young

The winningest coach in Rutgers basketball history, Young compiled a record of 239–116 as the school's head coach from 1973–1985, leading the Scarlet Knights to four NCAA tournament appearances, one Final Four, and three NITs, along with six twenty-win seasons. The University of Maryland graduate (he is in the Terps' Athletic Hall of Fame) compiled an overall record of 524–238 over thirty years as a college head coach, with stops at Catholic University, American, Rutgers, and Old Dominion. After retiring as a college coach, he became an assistant to Eddie Jordan, head coach of the Washington Wizards, from 2003–07.

Young passed away on March 20, 2022, at the age of eighty-nine. He is survived by his wife of sixty-seven years, Nancy, their children,

Tom Young Jr. and Tracy, and their grandchildren, TJ (Theodore Joseph), Sarah, Heather, Kayla, Madison, and Charles (Joey).

Joe Boylan

Boylan served as Tom Young's right-hand man and top assistant at Rutgers from 1973–85 before becoming an assistant athletic director at the school from 1985–91. He then spent nineteen years as the athletic director at Loyola University in his hometown of Baltimore before returning to Rutgers, where he then spent six years as an analyst on the Rutgers Radio Network. He was a graduate of Lafayette College.

Boylan passed away March 21, 2021, at the age of eighty-two. He is survived by his wife Molly, daughter Heather, son-in-law Dave Wojcik, and grandson, Jake.

John McFadden

A 1971 Rutgers graduate, the Springfield, Pennsylvania, native played for Dick Lloyd before joining his staff as an assistant for the 1971–72 season. Tom Young kept him on staff when he took over as head coach for the 1972–73 campaign. McFadden was a Rutgers assistant until 1978, when he made his move into the corporate world, with stops at the Xerox Corp., Merrill Lynch, Smith Barney, Wells Fargo and, most recently, Ameriprise Financial, where he serves as managing director, overseeing over $250 million in assets.

He has spent the past ten years as the assistant head coach for the Cherokee (NJ) High School girls' basketball team, helping the school to a 237–42 record. Over that span, Cherokee has captured five South Jersey Group 4 sectional titles and won a state championship in 2020.

John and his wife, Debbie, have two sons, Jack and Matt, a daughter, Melissa, and four grandchildren, Taylor, Aly, Tommy, and Maeve.

Art Perry

A Washington, DC, native and Air Force veteran, Perry was a guard for Tom Young's teams at American University from 1970–73 before injuries curtailed his playing career. He followed Young to Rutgers as a part-time assistant in 1973 while also working toward his degree in 1976. Following a two-year stint as an assistant at Connecticut, he returned to Rutgers as a full-time assistant coach from 1978–85. Perry then re-joined Young's staff as an assistant at Old Dominion from 1985–90, moving on to become an assistant at Maryland from 1990–96. Perry then became the head coach at Delaware State for one year before moving to American University, where he was the head coach from 1997–2000. He later worked for Nike before becoming the director of Hoops Central, an organization that advises players, coaches, and parents on matters relating to athletics and academics.

Perry's wife, Janis, is the daughter of Grammy Award-winning musician and composer Ernie Freeman.

PLAYERS

Abdel Anderson

Anderson, a native of Bellville, New Jersey, played in 120 games during his four-year Rutgers career, finishing with 1,459 points. After graduation, Anderson served as a probation officer in Middlesex County before becoming a detective in the Union County Prosecutor's Office, eventually being promoted to lieutenant. Following a brief retirement after twenty-six years in the Union County Prosecutor's Office, he worked for the NBA as a manager for security. He currently works for Homeland Security and plans to retire in December 2025.

Anderson has two children: Abdel Jr. and Brianna.

James Bailey

A second-team All-American in 1978, the 6–9 Bailey proved to be the missing piece when he was inserted into the starting lineup at center in the sixth game of the 1975–76 season. A native of Boston, he finished his career third on Rutgers's career scoring list with 2,034 points and is second in program history in rebounds with 1,047. He was selected sixth overall by the Seattle SuperSonics during the 1979 NBA draft and went on to play for five teams (the SuperSonics, New Jersey Nets, Houston Rockets, New York Knicks, and Phoenix Suns) during a nine-year NBA career.

From 1992 to 1995, Bailey was a National Hot Rod Association drag car race owner and operator. He then served as a national corporation executive (director/VP of human resources) for Foot Locker Inc. from 1993 to 2017.

He retired in 2017. He has a son, James Jr.

His No. 20 jersey was retired by Rutgers in 1993.

Mark Conlin

The only married player on Rutgers's 1975–76 roster, the Queens, New York, native appeared in 107 games for the Scarlet Knights from 1973–77 and started in twenty-nine of those games. Following graduation, Conlin began his career with the Xerox Corporation as a sales representative in New York City. In 1980, he returned to New Jersey to work for Harry Strauss & Sons in New Brunswick, then was hired to start up their business machines division, eventually rising to vice president. In 1990 he was hired by Canon USA to lead the New York City branch as vice president of sales.

In 2000, Mark returned to work for Xerox, where he spearheaded the New York/New Jersey branch as vice president. In 2014 he was promoted to president of the Xerox Foundation and CEO of corporate citizenship. He retired in 2018.

Conlin and his wife, Kathleen, have been married for fifty-three years. They had a son named Mark Jr., and they have a daughter named Katie. Their grandchildren are Brady Conlin and Brendan Streno.

Hollis Copeland

The fifth all-time leading scorer in Rutgers history with 1,769 points, Copeland is seventh all-time in rebounding and was an honorable mention All-American in 1977. A third-round pick by the Denver Nuggets in the 1978 NBA draft, Copeland went on to play two years for the New York Knicks with Patrick Ewing before retiring from the NBA.

After basketball, Hollis became a hospital care investigator, salesman, and stockbroker. He was inducted into the Rutgers Athletics Hall of Fame in 1996. He has also been a very significant member of the Rutgers community for two decades, serving on the university's board of directors for nineteen years and currently serving as a member of the board of governors.

Copeland and his wife, Delena, have been married for forty-two years. They have two children, Yasmin and Julian.

Mike Dabney

A native of East Orange, New Jersey, Dabney was a four-year starter and the second-leading scorer (19.1 ppg to Phil Sellers's 19.2 ppg) on Rutgers's Final Four team, earning honorable mention All-America honors that season. He is still fourth on the school's career scoring list with 1,902 points, and his 111 steals in 1975–76 set a single-season program record. Twice during the 1975–76 season he set the school's single-game record with nine steals. He was drafted in the third round of the 1976 NBA draft by the Los Angeles Lakers and was the last cut that year.

After leaving Los Angeles, he became a financial analyst and sold municipal bonds in New Jersey. In 1978 he went to camp with the Boston Celtics and appeared to have made the team before suffering a torn hamstring that essentially dashed his NBA hopes.

In 1979, Mike moved back to Southern California, where he continued in the financial world and met his future wife, Jolette.

The couple then moved back to New Jersey, where Mike worked in financial services before joining UPS as an international sales representative. He worked for Wells Fargo before retiring.

Mike remains active in the New Jersey school system and was inducted into the Rutgers Athletic Hall of Fame in 1995.

The Dabneys have six children: Vaughn, Jasaan, Maya, Ashley, Olivia, and the late Christina.

Steve Hefele

Immediately following graduation, Hefele coached the varsity basketball team at Sayreville (NJ) High School. He taught health, physical education and driver's education there for two years before playing professionally in Belgium for a year. From there he continued his basketball career as a player and coach at St. Truiden, Belgium. He then moved back to the US and joined the staff of Springfield College, where he taught fellowship and coached the jayvee basketball team from 1983–85.

Hefele then spent thirty-three years teaching and coaching basketball, football, and softball at Friends Academy on Long Island before retiring in 2018.

Steve and his wife, Lynn, have two children, Harrison and TJ.

Eddie Jordan

Known for his quickness (hence the nickname "Fast Eddie"), Jordan played in 116 games as Rutgers's point guard from 1973–77. He is ninth on the school's career scoring list with 1,632 points and is still the program's all-time leader in assists. A second-round pick by the Cleveland Cavaliers in the 1977 NBA draft, Jordan played for four teams (Cavaliers, New Jersey Nets, Portland Trailblazers, and Los Angeles Lakers) during an NBA career that spanned from 1977–84 and was a member of the 1982 Los Angeles Lakers's NBA championship team. While with the Nets in 1979, he led the NBA in steals. Jordan went on to be the head coach of the Sacramento Kings, Washington Wizards, and Philadelphia 76ers before returning to his alma mater to serve as Rutgers's head coach from 2013–16. He then served as an assistant coach with the Charlotte Hornets in 2017–18.

He was inducted into the Rutgers Athletics Hall of Fame in 1994.

Jordan retired in 2018 and currently lives in Charlotte, North Carolina, where he gets to play golf four days a week. Jordan and his wife, Janica, have six children: Paul, Eddie II (who played football at Rutgers), Justin, Matthew, Jawon, and Skylar.

Jeff Kleinbaum

Known as "Mr. 100" during Rutgers's Final Four season, I became the head basketball coach and assistant baseball coach at Spotswood (NJ) High School, where I also taught American history and economics shortly after graduating from Rutgers in 1976. After five years at Spotswood (Middlesex County Coach of the Year in 1979), I then moved to Union (NJ) High School, where I taught in the social studies department and coached the varsity boys basketball team from 1982–84.

After leaving education in 1984, I worked on Wall Street from 1985–1995. I then returned to teach history and economics and coach the varsity boys basketball team at Middletown North (NJ) High School from 1995–2000. In 2001, I moved to Whippany Park (NJ) High School, where I taught and coached basketball for twenty-three years, earning Morris County Coach of the Year honors in 2003. A native of Queens, New York, I was drafted by the New York Mets out of high school. I also coached varsity baseball at Whippany Park High School before retiring in July of 2024.

I appeared in 106 games during my Rutgers career.

My wife, Deborah, and I have two daughters, Laura and Michelle, and a son-in-law, Mike.

Stan Nance

Following a Rutgers career that saw him appear in sixty-four games, the Washington, DC, native became a college coach, serving as an assistant at Rutgers, St. Peter's, Boston College, VCU, Miami (FL), Old Dominion, West Virginia, Hartford, Northeastern, and Rutgers again. He has been the senior associate director of athletics and recruiting coordinator at Emerson College, a Division III school in Boston, since 2002.

Stan and his wife, Alethea A. McFarlane, have a son, Darnell James.

Mike Palko

Mike started the first five games and played in twenty-two during Rutgers's 1975–76 Final Four season after starting nineteen games the year before. Overall, he played in eighty-eight games during his four years at Rutgers. A native of Hackettstown, New Jersey, he went on to become a teacher for thirty-two years, thirty-one at Randolph (NJ) High School, where he taught history, economics, social psychology, and propaganda. He was a charter member of the Randolph High School Teachers Select Choir for fifteen years. He returned to school in 2008, earning a master's degree in secondary education.

Mike served as the basketball coach at Hackettstown High School, Randolph High School, Warren Hills Regional High School, and North Warren Regional High School for twenty-five years before retiring from teaching and coaching in 2009.

He and his wife, Patty, have two married sons, Michael Jr. and James, and two grandchildren, Matthew and Madison.

Bruce Scherer

Following graduation, the Parsippany, New Jersey, native, who appeared in fifty-six games during his Rutgers career, worked for A. B. Dick Company from 1976–78. From 1978–80, he worked for Lebhar-Friedman, selling advertising on the East Coast.

Looking to reduce his travel after he met the love of his life, Daryl, Scherer changed industries and joined Guardsmark, a company providing uniformed guards and investigation services in New York. He remained in the security industry for the next thirty-three years.

In 2014, Scherer joined ASG, a turnkey provider to the telecom industry. As director of client relations, he was instrumental in helping the company grow from $10 million in sales to $150 million and was a key player in the company's growth from 100 employees to 750. He remained at ASG until December 2024, when he retired.

Bruce and Daryl have four children: Walter, Peter, Madeline, and Lana, and three grandchildren with another on the way.

Phil Sellers

The most accomplished player in Rutgers basketball history, Sellers is still the school's career leader in points (2,399) and rebounds (1,115)—fifty years after his last game. The 6–4 Brooklyn, New York, native was a two-time All-American and the driving force in the program's emergence as a national program. He was taken in the third round of the NBA draft by the Detroit Pistons and also played professionally in the Netherlands. His No. 12 jersey was retired by Rutgers in 1988, and he was inducted into the school's Athletic Hall of Fame in 1993.

Sellers returned to Rutgers as an assistant coach for four years before going into the private sector, working as an office manager for Margaretten Mortgage Company and then later with JPMorganChase. He went on to work for the Northeast Private Client Group until his retirement in 2018.

Sellers passed away on September 19, 2023, at the age of sixty-nine. He is survived by his wife, Patricia; his son, Phillip A. Sellers; his daughter, Kendra Michelle Palmer; and his grandchildren, Khloe Michelle Palmer, Kamryn Marie Palmer, Elijah Phillip Palmer, and London Arya Rose Coveney-Sellers.

1975–76 ROSTER, FINAL STATISTICS, AND RESULTS

1975-76 Rutgers Basketball Roster

No.	Name	Pos.	Class	Ht.	Wt.	Hometown/HS
54	Abdel Anderson	F	Fr.	6-7	185	Belleville, N.J. (Belleville)
20	James Bailey	C	Fr.	6-9	195	Boston, MA (Xaverian)
42	Mark Conlin	G	Jr.	6-2	175	Queens, N.Y. (Bishop Reilly)
34	Hollis Copeland	F	So.	6-6	180	Trenton, N.J. (Ewing)
32	Mike Dabney	G	Sr.	6-4	180	East Orange, N.J. (East Orange)
50	Steve Hefele	G/F	So.	6-5	190	East Rockaway, N.Y. (East Rockaway)
30	Ed Jordan	G	Jr.	6-2	160	Washington, D.C. (Archbishop Carroll)
44	Jeff Kleinbaum	G/F	Sr.	6-2	190	Queens, N.Y. (Van Buren)
22	Stan Nance	G	So.	6-3	170	Washington, D.C. (Spingarn)
52	Mike Palko	C	Sr.	6-7	200	Hackettstown, N.J. (Hackettstown)
24	Bruce Scherer	C	Sr.	6-7	200	Parsippany, N.J. (Parsippany Hills)
13	Phil Sellers	F	Sr.	6-5	200	Brooklyn, N.Y. (Thomas Jefferson)

Head coach: Tom Young

Assistant coaches: Joe Boylan, John McFadden, Art Perry

1975-76
THE PERFECT SEASON

SCARLET

RESULTS

Rutgers 100, Bentley 60
Rutgers 81, Purdue 73
Rutgers 119, Seton Hall 93
Rutgers 104, Boston College 82
Rutgers 95, Penn 80
Rutgers 96, Connecticut 83
Rutgers 95, Temple 62
Rutgers 96, The Citadel 73*
Rutgers 94, Georgia Tech 87*
Rutgers 91, Stetson 70
Rutgers 93, Fordham 55
Rutgers 94, Columbia 65
Rutgers 105, Bucknell 82
Rutgers 102, Lehigh 87
Rutgers 113, Lafayette 79
Rutgers 102, Pitt 71
Rutgers 75, Princeton 62
Rutgers 86, West Virginia 76
Rutgers 86, Navy 71

Rutgers 110, Delaware 87
Rutgers 92, Manhattan 81 (OT)
Rutgers 93, Syracuse 80
Rutgers 94, American 79
Rutgers 100, W & M 90
Rutgers 103, LIU 87
Rutgers 85, St. Bonaventure 80
Rutgers 104, LIU 76#
Rutgers 70, St. John's 67#
Rutgers 54, Princeton 53+
Rutgers 93, Connecticut 79+
Rutgers 91, VMI 75+
Michigan 86, Rutgers 70++
UCLA 106, Rutgers 92++
*Poinsettia Classic
#ECAC Metropolitan Tournament
@NCAA
+Eastern Regionals
++NCAA Final Four

FINAL BASKETBALL STATISTICS

33-Game Totals
OVERALL RECORD: 31-2
Home: 10-0; Away 21-2

ECAC MET CHAMPIONS
NCAA EASTERN REGIONAL CHAMPIONS
NCAA FINAL FOUR

		G-GS	MIN	FG-FGA	PCT	FT-FTA	PCT	RBD-AVG	PTS-AVG	HIGH
12	Phil Sellers	33-33	1075	243-543	44.8	148-203	72.9	337-10.2	634-19.2	36
32	Mike Dabney	33-33	1037	272-573	47.5	85-111	76.6	148- 4.6	629-19.1	33
30	Ed Jordan	33-32	939	187-397	47.1	90-113	79.6	102- 3.1	464-14.1	23
34	Hollis Copeland	33-32	964	197-392	50.3	32- 63	50.8	220- 6.7	426-12.9	22
54	Abdel Anderson	33	662	112-218	51.4	86-114	75.4	144- 4.4	310- 9.4	21
20	James Bailey	33-28	790	121-240	50.4	40- 68	58.8	233- 7.1	282- 8.5	23
50	Steve Hefele	32-1	371	51-115	44.3	16- 41	39.0	83- 2.6	118- 3.7	14
44	Jeff Kleinbaum	27	143	29-61	47.5	16- 35	45.7	25- 0.9	74- 2.7	11
42	Mark Conlin	32-1	325	25-43	58.1	18- 25	72.0	26- 0.8	68- 2.1	10
52	Mike Palko	22-5	216	17-33	51.5	7- 14	50.0	62- 2.8	41- 1.9	5
24	Bruce Scherer	13	51	12-29	41.4	4- 5	80.0	23- 1.8	28- 2.2	6
22	Stan Nance	14	44	6-25	24.0	4- 9	44.4	10- 0.7	16- 1.1	4
	Team rebounds included in total					166				
	(Deadball rebounds not in total)					107				
	RUTGERS TOTALS	33		1272-2669	47.7	546-801	68.2	1578-47.8	3090-93.6	
	OPPONENTS TOTALS	33		1013-2282	44.0	511-726	70.3	1356-41.1	2537-76.9	
	Team rebounds included in total					146				
	(Deadball rebounds not in total)					101				

ASSISTS: Jordan 174, Dabney 117, Sellers 106, Conlin 46, Copeland 50, Hefele 29, Anderson 21, Bailey 19, Kleinbaum 6, Palko 4, Nance 2, Scherer 3
STEALS: Dabney 110, Jordan 100, Sellers 62, Bailey 41, Copeland 28, Anderson 17, Conlin 15, Hefele 15, Palko 7, Kleinbaum 6, Scherer 2, Nance 1
BLOCKED SHOTS: Bailey 98, Copeland 31, Sellers 19, Anderson 13, Dabney 11, Hefele 9, Palko 2, Jordan 1
Phil Sellers — All-time career scorer (2399); rebounder (1112)
Mike Dabney — Third on all-time scoring list (1902)
Ed Jordan — 10th on all-time scoring list (1236)

21

ACKNOWLEDGMENTS

NEVER HAVING WRITTEN A BOOK before, I knew I would be leaning on many people to make this the best it could be. People have been waiting for a book on this topic for a very long time, and I did not want to disappoint.

First and foremost, I want to thank my teammates for allowing me to call on them day and night to get the information I needed. I felt like I was transported back to 1976 and they promised at the beginning to do anything I needed and then delivered just that. I also want to thank them for enriching my life as only family can do.

Although each player pulled together like we had fifty years earlier, Bruce Scherer needs some special recognition. Four days after I told my teammates that I was writing a book about all of us, Bruce suffered a stroke. Thankfully, he is making a full recovery, but those first two months after his stroke were very difficult on everyone, especially his wonderful loving family. The thing that was incredible about Bruce's recovery was that he continued to help me with the book and was able to find a tremendous amount of information and pictures that I used. You are an incredible human being, Bruce, and we all are thrilled for your good health.

Tom Young and Joe Boylan passed away before the book was started, but assistant coaches John McFadden and Art Perry provided important perspectives that only they could give. It would not have been accurate if it weren't for them, so a great deal of credit belongs there.

I approached Tom Luicci to help me write a coherent piece of work, and he did that and more. I went to Tom early on because as a student at

Rutgers in the 1970s, he was the coeditor of *The Daily Targum* during the Final Four year. Thank you, Tom, for having the patience and skill to keep me on the right track and make sure I never strayed from writing an accurate and interesting account of our special year.

I never knew how critical it was to have a good publisher while trying to put together a project like this. To use a term from another sport I liked to play, I hit a home run when Roger Brooks of American Real Publishing agreed to take on that role. Roger guided me from the first day we spoke until the book was completely done, and he is still making sure things go well for me. Most importantly, the team he put together on my behalf was the best I could ever imagine. I can't thank enough Connor Grant, the Managing Partner; Tara Monaco, Client Success Manager; and Debra Hartmann, Managing Editor, for their kindness, professionalism, and expertise. This Dream Team of publishing professionals is one of the greatest teams I've ever been a part of, and I have been a part of quite a few great ones.

John Harper, my friend for fifty years and one of the best sports journalists in the US, let me know early on that he would be available to help and has done just that. There were many times I got extremely stressed out and he was there to calm me down just as he had done for ten years when he helped me coach basketball at Whippany Park High School. Sometimes, I would get a bit upset with a referee. He saved me from more technical fouls than anyone could imagine. Thanks, John.

Kathleen Conlin, Mark's wife, has worked in the Rutgers Athletic Department for over thirty-two years—ten in the Athletic Directors office and twenty-two in Marketing and Promotions. More importantly to our basketball team, she has been our "house mother" by making sure we kept up with each other for things like birthdays, anniversaries, and special events. For this book, she has compiled more than seventy pictures for me to look through, and without them, I would not have had nearly the quality of the book that eventually was published.

One of the wonderful things about writing this book fifty years after the fact was the number of people I reconnected with. I was looking for pictures and trying to find people who were at games and that is how I ran into Nancy Bechtold (Cramer). She was the captain of the cheerleaders in 1976, and her mother kept an incredible scrapbook of articles and pictures of every game, as well as stories written by journalists who followed us. She was kind enough to send me her very valuable memory book, and it was a tremendous help all the way through the writing period. I also met a wonderful woman named Ann Marie Gurda, who was sixteen years old in 1976, and she gave me a wonderful memory scrapbook as well. I would not have been able to get the very necessary information to write about the specific games and interviews players and coaches gave if it weren't for Nancy and Ann Marie.

Al Reicheg, the president of the Court Club, was one of the first people to volunteer to help me when he was made aware that I was writing this book. He helped get the word out to hundreds of people to let them know I was looking for their memories of the 1975–76 season and the ones that appear in the book are just a sampling of the dozens I received. The memories I included in the book made the entire project much more rich and rewarding. I would like to thank each of you and let you all know how deeply indebted I am. Thank you, Elizebeth "Betsy" Shott, Robert Merker, Chris Jennings. Dr. Alan Venook, Ann Marie Gorda, Cliff Smith, Darryl Gurney, Mike Brill, John Wooding, Bruce Beck, and Brian Perkins for those heartwarming stories that made the time period come alive from the perspective of those who were there and loved being part of it all.

Speaking of Brian Perkins, he has been extremely instrumental in helping get this book written and into the public's hands. We call him the thirteenth player on the team because he was recruited by Rutgers the same year all the seniors on the Final Four were recruited, but the athletic program only had one more scholarship to give that year, and they gave it to Phil Sellers.

Although he didn't actually play on varsity (he played on the last two junior varsity teams Rutgers ever had), his expertise from his thirty-two years at Johnson & Johnson as Worldwide Chairman, Consumer Pharmaceuticals & Nutritional as well as being a member of the Executive Committee was, and is, immeasurable.

Special thanks go to Dick Vitale of *ESPN Sports* and former assistant coach at Rutgers and head coach of the University of Detroit and the Detroit Pistons; Bill Raftery of *CBS Sports* and former head coach of the Seton Hall Pirates; Ed Jordan, one of the players on our team as well as a nine-year veteran of the NBA, the former head coach at Rutgers, and head coach of the Sacramento Kings, Washington Wizards, and Philadelphia 76ers; and Bruce Beck of *NBC Sports* and a sports journalist for the past fifty years. They were nice enough to read the book and provide the endorsements that appear in it. Because some very important people from our journey as a team had passed away, I reached out to people close to them. I give my heartfelt thanks to Tom Young Jr., Nancy Young, Molly Boylan, Ryke Suydam, and Robyn Suydam for providing tremendous insight of their loved one's feelings and actions back then.

Mike MacDonald provided information about several people I needed to contact. He always responded to my requests with speed and accuracy, and I thank him for that.

It was very important to get the point of view of some of our opponents to have their perspective on games we played. I thank Frank Alagia from St. Johns, Armond Hill from Princeton, and Jim Baron from St. Bonaventure for their honest appraisal of the events of 1975–76.

Finally, I wish to thank my family. They each were incredibly supportive from the very first minute I told them that this was my dream and they helped me in immeasurable ways. Lynn and Alan, you not only helped me find a terrific publisher but kept me thinking positively at all times, even when my spirits wavered a little bit. Laura, Michelle, and Mike, you kept reminding me that this project was well within my grasp and in the end, you were 100 percent correct. To my nieces and nephews, thanks for making me laugh every day as I wrote and wrote and wrote. Maryanne, Laura, Anthony, and Peter, thanks for keeping me humble when I sometimes got too big for my britches. And Deborah, thanks for being my partner through all of this. We were not together when this Final Four was played, but based on all the stories you've heard over the years, you know what happened as much or more than I do.

I love every single person I have just mentioned and truly hope you all enjoy the end result.

ABOUT THE AUTHORS

Jeff Kleinbaum attended Rutgers University, where he played on the famous Final Four basketball team and captained the baseball team in its first NCAA appearance in nearly ten years, both in 1976.

He went on to a forty-year teaching and coaching career, interrupted only by a ten-year stint on Wall Street. While coaching high school basketball and baseball, he was named both Middlesex County Coach of the Year and Morris County Coach of the Year.

Jeff retired in 2024 and lasted a mere five months before launching a new career as an author. He lives with his wife Deborah and golden retriever Scarlett in Florham Park, New Jersey.

Tom Luicci covered college football, college basketball, and horse racing for *The Star-Ledger* of Newark, NJ, for thirty-five years (1979-2014) and was named New Jersey Sportswriter of the Year by the National Sports Media Association a record ten times.

He has covered every major college football bowl game and thirty consecutive Final Fours since 1980.

A 1977 Rutgers College graduate, Tom was a three-time sports editor of *The Daily Targum*, the student newspaper, and covered the 1976 Final Four as a student. He is currently the Media Director at Monmouth Park Racetrack.